WHY DOES MY DOG DO THAT?!

LIFE IN A MULTI-SPECIES HOME EXPLAINED

WHY DOES MY DOG DO THAT?!

LIFE IN A MULTI-SPECIES HOME EXPLAINED

DELORES CARTER

SEE SPOT LEARN PUBLISHING

Editor: Eileen Anderson

Cover design: Anastasia Zein

See Spot Learn Publishing
7701 Winans Lake Rd
Brighton, MI 48116
info@seespotlearnpublishing.com

Why Does My Dog Do That?! Life in a Multi-Species Home Explained/Delores Carter. 1st edition

ISBN 979-8-9896846-0-1 Paperback

ISBN 979-8-9896846-1-8 E-book

Muse (2008-2019)
For Muse, the deaf and blind Great Dane who changed my world forever. You taught me to see the world from a dog's perspective. You made me really think about the question "Why does my dog do that?" Then you showed me how great life can be when we humans step back and let dogs do doggie things.

CONTENTS

INTRODUCTION

Why do you have a dog? Why do I have a dog? Honestly, before I married my husband 35 years ago, I didn't want a dog. I liked cats (and I still do). Nope, no dogs for me. It broke my husband's heart. After many conversations and a little coaxing, I thought maybe a dog would be okay. For the kids, you know. A family needs a dog to be whole, right? I wasn't completely convinced. And then I met a greyhound. Sox was my first heart dog, the one who set me on my path and made way for the dozens of dogs who have shared my home over the years.

While this book isn't just about my journey, you'll read about many of the dogs who have lived with my family: the family dogs, the foster dogs, and the fosters who stayed. This is the book that relates how the dogs (and cats, rabbits, guinea pigs, hamsters, lizards, chickens, and fish) in my life opened my eyes to living in a multi-species home. It's really about my learning to see life from a different perspective, a non-human perspective. I'd like to think that, with the help of the other species in my life, I've become a better human: more empathetic, more interesting, and more accepting.

Although there have been multiple species in my home over the years, this book focuses on the canine-human relationship. The principles of creating a home where humans and different species of companion pets (i.e., cats, rabbits, guinea pigs, etc.) live peacefully together, while meeting the needs of each species are the same regardless of the non-human species in your home.

CANINES AND HUMANS: INTERSPECIES CONNECTION

Dogs and people share a long and fascinating history together. Over time, dogs and people learned to work together, enriching each other's lives. Dogs were valued for their ability to partner in human activities like hunting, herding, and protecting. Notice that being alone at home is not on that list. Life has changed for our contemporary canine companions. Often dogs are valued for doing nothing. Literally nothing, just staying home all day, often alone. Doing nothing is incompatible with the canine species' living a normal life. And here we are at the starting point of much of the tension in the human-canine home. Dogs are often prized for doing nothing, which is fundamentally incompatible with doggie DNA.

New industries have emerged to help people with their bored and lonely dogs. We have doggie daycare, dog walkers, and doggie puzzle toys. These all have their place and can be beneficial. But notice – none of these activities replaces the tasks dogs were once prized for: working alongside their human companions. For the remainder of the book, we'll look at why dogs do the things they do, why they need to do doggie things, and how we, as their guardians, can meet them where they are. We'll begin by "thinking like a dog."

PART ONE
THINK LIKE A DOG

1

LIVING IN YOUR WORLD: YOUR DOG'S PERSPECTIVE

This may sound obvious, but do you realize your dog is not human? Sometimes we forget. We attribute thoughts, feelings, and needs to our dogs that have nothing to do with being a dog. We all do it at some point. When my dog takes something from the counter, I may accuse her of theft and be upset, but she's not a thief (more on that later). She was doing a doggie thing. It shouldn't surprise me when my dog acts like a dog. But sometimes, it does. She's a dog . . . I'm a human.

Most of the time, our human and canine worlds blend beautifully. That's one of the many reasons people invite dogs into their hearts and homes. When things don't blend so wonderfully, then there is tension, and we're unhappy. We're left wondering, "Why does he do that?" Our dogs are unhappy, too. They're wondering, "Why does my human do that?" Our dogs want nothing more than peace. And really, we do, too.

One way to achieve that peaceful, multi-species home is to understand the other point of view. Setting aside our own cultural and biological norms (it's hard!) and seeing the world through our dogs' eyes (and ears, mouth, and feet) helps us better understand why our dogs do some of the strange and sometimes frustrating things they do. I believe it also helps us see the humorous side of our dogs. It relieves tension between the person and the dog. It takes us a step closer to a peaceful home.

Sometimes, we apply our human perspective and morals to our pets. Sometimes that works out. Sometimes it doesn't. Expecting our dogs to understand and adapt to some of our human behaviors and social norms can leave them confused. We can inadvertently set up a no-win situation, leading us and our dogs down an unhappy path.

So, what does the world look like from our dogs' perspective? It may be very different than what you were taught, what you believe, or what you see in the media. Dogs are dogs, and they need to do doggie things. Let's explore some of the ways our homes and our human perspective affect our dogs' opportunity to express their doggie nature.

A GOOD HOME . . . (THE PLACE YOUR DOG SHOULD FEEL FREE TO BE A DOG)

Rescue groups, shelters, breeders, veterinarians, and people on the street generally agree that every companion pet should have a good home. But what is a good home? The answer depends on many things: culture, the species of your companion pet, whether you live in a high-rise apartment or a farm. People have their own standards that may not match the standards of others. A good home is one that meets the needs of the dog, where your dog can be okay. How do you know if your home meets your dog's needs? Let's start with a home tour.

HOME TOUR . . . (LOOKING THROUGH THE EYES OF YOUR DOG)

The day finally arrived. Your new dog is coming home. You're prepared: food and water bowls, a new leash, a new collar, a dog bed, and a few toys. It's an exciting moment for everyone. But, when you brought your dog home, did you wonder what your dog might think of her new home? Maybe you brought home a puppy from a breeder or an adolescent from a rescue group, or perhaps you inherited the dog now sitting in your living room. Whatever the path was, how does your dog feel about her new home? Is it dog friendly?

Let's look at your home through your dog's eyes. I want you to really look at your home from your dog's line of sight. How tall is your dog? When your dog walks into a room, what's at eye level? Is anything interesting (from your dog's perspective)? Are those things safe or unsafe? I have two dogs in my house. Ursa is a Great Dane. Her eye level is slightly higher than 3 feet off the ground. When she walks into the kitchen, she can see everything on the counter, and she can drink out of the kitchen sink. She can 'sit' at the kitchen table and eat from our plates with ease. She doesn't need to jump up on the counter or the table to see what's up there.

Roadie is our other canine companion. He's much shorter than Ursa. His worldview is about 2 feet off the ground. When he walks into the kitchen, he has an excellent view of the cabinet doors and the seats of the chairs at the table. If he were curious about what was on the countertop, he would need to jump up and place his paws on the counter to have a look around.

Both of my dogs would happily get their own snacks off the counter. I might hear Roadie jump on the counter, alerting me to counter-surfing activity. Ursa could walk by, grab a snack, and keep going, and I'd never hear her. Actually, Ursa (and most of the dogs I've lived with) have done just that at one time or another. They are eager to scan the environment in hopes of an opportunity to forage. That's what dogs do. It's part of their DNA. If my expectation is that dogs will act like dogs, and if I leave my freshly toasted bagel on the counter, then walk into another room, get distracted, and return to the kitchen 15 minutes later, my bagel might be gone. Is my dog bad? No. She's just being a dog.

If I wanted my kitchen to be truly dog friendly, then I would need to allow them to forage freely. That would include counter-surfing, trashcan digging, and grazing off the table. Think I'm joking? Not at all. When we're really thinking from the dog's perspective, we need to accept, however grudgingly, that what the dog thinks is perfectly normal may not be acceptable to our human sensibilities. Here's where we need to compromise so that our dog's needs are met, and our counter-tops remain drool-free.

If I want to prevent normal doggie behavior in the kitchen, like foraging, then I need to set it up so my dog has few opportunities to practice foraging (counter-surfing and trashing). Even with nothing of interest on the counter, Ursa will peruse the counter. Is that naughty? No. She's exploring her environment, on the lookout for anything that has changed since her last kitchen patrol. She regularly patrols the house, looking for changes. Any change in the environment, in her mind, needs to be investigated. Normal dog behavior. It's in my best interest to ensure that regular kitchen patrol duties, like counter-surfing, are dog-safe (i.e., no food on the counter that could reinforce counter-surfing behavior and nothing that could harm them if they decided to have a nibble).

Leaving the kitchen, let's head to the living room. What is

your dog's experience in the living room? What is a living room, from your dog's perspective?

In my home, the living room is where we spend the most time together. The living room, which is on the main floor, is generally quiet. It's a good place to rest or read a book. The dogs use the living room a little differently than the humans do. They watch the world through the picture window while lounging comfortably on the sectional. This is Ursa's "observation station." She is the first to know when anyone drives up the driveway. She takes her job seriously. UPS? Amazon? Fed Ex? WOOF WOOF! Friend or family driving up to the house? WOOF WOOF WOOF paired with prancing and dancing. On sunny days, she can sunbathe in the middle of the floor. In the cold winter months, she can snuggle up in blankets on the sectional, chair, or one of the dog beds. It really is a great place to alert the family to potential external threats, comfortably, of course.

Roadie, on the other hand, treats the living room like a "nap zone." He doesn't care what delivery truck is in the driveway as long as his nap isn't interrupted. He has his own spot on the sectional as well as a favored dog bed. The living room does give him easy access to guests coming into the house so he can perform his official greeting duty. No one comes into the house without greeting Roadie.

The living room is also a prime indoor space for canine play. Big dogs play in a big way! The furniture literally moved when my adolescent dogs had bouts of the zoomies. What is furniture, after all, but soft, cushioned obstacles? Our current furniture arrangement allows dogs to leap over the back of an armchair or to use the end table as a viewing platform.

Couches are great places for hiding a bone and then digging it back up. The sectional provides a cushioned obstacle for the dogs to bank on when zooming around the living room.

When Roadie was younger, he would stand on the arm of the sectional, which made him equal in height to the Great Danes. Really, we humans aren't very creative when using our furniture. We sit or maybe lie down. And we stay still. The point is, your dog's use of the living room and its furnishings may leave you scratching your head and asking yourself, "Why does my dog do that?"

Author's note: I don't encourage any of the dogs to leap over the furniture. The thought of an injury and a long recovery makes my heart stop. Unfortunately, my feelings have zero effect on an adolescent dog in full zoomie mode. Dogs doing doggie things may cause your heart to skip a beat.

Next up on our tour is the home office. People who work from home offices need to decide if their dog can be in the office during working hours. My dogs spend time in my office, hanging out while I'm working. It's not uncommon for Ursa to join me for a Zoom call. My office is dog friendly. When either or both of the dogs wander into the office, they have options that promote calm behavior, which is what I want when I'm working at my desk. There are two dog beds and a couch the dogs can lounge on, a dog water fountain, and things to chew. It's set up to encourage quiet, calm behavior. Tug toys and squeaky toys are not allowed. That's one way I set up the dogs to be successful in my office. The are no options to annoy me with a squeaky toy while I'm on the phone with a client. When Ursa or Roadie gives me a nudge, usually it's to let me know they need to go outside or that it's time for our walk. That's reasonable. If they want to play tug with each other, they have options. The toy boxes in the living room, family room, and bedroom have a variety of toys for tugging. The only things for my dogs to do in my office are chewing and resting. Both are quiet activities that allow me to work and spend time with my dogs.

We've taken a brief home tour, but we haven't talked about what a home is. What does "home" mean to you? To your dog? My home is my safe space. It's where I retreat from the world to rest and recharge. I've arranged my home to meet my needs. But what about my dogs? What do they have to do in each room? In most of the rooms in my house, there are things to do that I enjoy: books to read, music to listen to, windows to watch the world. While my dogs spend a lot of time napping or watching the world out the window, I know they also need doggy things to do. I could leave them to figure out how to entertain themselves. What they choose may or may not be acceptable to me.

Alternatively, I can provide options for them. That's why I have toy boxes for the dogs in the rooms where they are likely to be active. There are toy boxes in the living room, one in the family room, and one in my bedroom. In each toy box, there is a variety of things for the dogs to choose from: hard chews (bull horns, bones), squeaky toys, tug toys, balls, and plush toys. I teach my dogs to get a toy after they alert bark. Keeping a toy box near areas where barking is likely (front door, windows) gives my dogs quick access to a toy, which decreases the amount of time spent barking. When someone comes into my home, directing an excited dog to "get your toy" helps the barking dog engage in an activity to burn off a little energy.

Even though there are dog beds and toy boxes for the dogs, some aspects of my home are not dog friendly for puppies or dogs with mobility issues. Living in a quad-level home with three sets of stairs inside the house and no way to get outside without using stairs makes life more difficult for my 14-year-old dog, who has arthritis. Getting puppies outside to potty also requires traversing multiple sets of steps inside the house and then getting outside to the grass. My senior dog sometimes needs help getting up the steps. Every home has some challenges for dogs. Making small adjustments can help your dog feel like his home is safe for him, too. Some of the things I've done to accommodate dogs over the years are putting down rugs to prevent slipping on hard floors, gating off rooms to promote house-training success, covering windows to promote a calm indoor environment, and using dog-proof trash cans.

THE GREAT (FENCED) OUTDOORS

Think for a moment about the outdoor space attached to your home. Perhaps you have a patio or balcony. You may have a common space that both people and pets use. You may have a yard, with or without a physical fence. You know the boundaries and the rules. But, what does your dog think of the outdoor space attached to your home? How does your dog experience her outdoor space?

The yard is another part of our family's living space. My dogs enjoy spending time outside, especially if I'm outside with them. We all enjoy relaxing on the deck in the backyard. When I work in my garden, the dogs are often outside with me. Creating a living space that is compatible with natural dog behavior improves your dog's quality of life while decreasing typically undesirable but perfectly normal doggie behaviors. One of my favorite activities is watching my dogs while they're in the yard. I can sit for hours observing and pondering the question, "Why does she do that?" The reason I can relax and take time to observe them in the yard is that I've intentionally created a space that is dog safe. I generally don't need to intervene while the dogs explore the backyard. Answering the question, "What do I want my dog to do," prevents human reactivity toward normal dog behavior. Rather than saying "no" frequently and becoming exasperated when your dog persists, you get to say, "Yes, here are your options." By the way, "No" is not a behavior. But more about that later. With that in mind, the yard needs to be as dog friendly as the house.

I have a few fallen trees in the fenced backyard, a repurposed tractor tire filled with dirt, and a brush pile. The dogs dig in the tire, sniff around the fallen trees and brush pile, and leap over the fallen trees. They also have elevated cots on the deck, which help them stay cool while lounging in the sun. Taking time to create a place for the dogs to just be dogs keeps our outdoor time relaxed and pleasant. I don't need to be concerned with what the dogs might get into. The only "rule" in the backyard is "Don't go out the gate unless given permission." Other than that, it is the dog's domain. Bark at the squirrels? Ok. Do zoomies? Go ahead. Chase the leaves? Knock yourself out.

Being in the garden or front yard is different. There are places in our front yard and garden where digging is allowed. Why? For two reasons. First, dogs dig, especially when it's hot outside. Digging a spot in the dirt and then lying down is one way dogs are able to cool off on hot summer days, which is exactly when I'll be spending the most time in the front yard. Second, if my dog is digging in a "legal" digging spot that I created, then I know where my dog is. But isn't a hole in the ground unsightly or unsafe? It can be. But here's a solution. When we moved into our current home a few years ago, I spent time observing my dogs in the yard. Where did they like to go? What was interesting to them? When I identified a few favored spots, I let the dogs settle in and dig a hole. Then I landscaped around the hole. Roadie has three favored dig spots: one under the front steps, one on the side of the house in a corner, hidden by a hibiscus plant, and the third on the other side of the house, now hidden by a euonymus bush. A simple solution that made everyone happy – I got to buy new plants (yes!), the dogs have "legal" dig spots (yes!), and we enjoy the yard from our unique species-specific perspectives (yes!).

Because I love having the dogs in the front yard, I need to think about their safety. I can teach the dogs the boundaries, or I can tether them. I actually do both. While the dogs are learning the boundaries, they are on a long lead. No long line is needed if I'm out in the front yard and my attention is focused on the dogs. But, if I'm cleaning the pond, pulling weeds, or otherwise engaged in yard work, the dogs might wear a lead. The long lead reaches as far as their boundary, which means they can go almost anywhere in the front yard. Once the boundaries are learned, then the lead is no longer needed. At the moment, Roadie is free to be out in the yard without a lead. Ursa still wears a lead if I know I'll be distracted. The dogs are never left in the front yard or garden unattended. That combination of management and training allows my dogs and me to be together in the yard.

What is management? Management means adjusting the environment to prevent my dog from practicing undesirable behavior. Management is key to training success, in my mind. There are situations where management is a more efficient solution than training. While teaching my dog to greet people, I might use a baby gate to separate her from guests entering our home. In other situations, I'll use what I call lifestyle management. For example, to prevent unnecessary competition over food, I feed each of my dogs in their crates, again managing the environment to prevent practicing unwanted behavior.

CAR RIDES . . . (FUN OR FRIGHTENING FOR YOUR DOG?)

While not technically your living space, your dog will probably need to be in your car at some point. Can your dog get into and out of your car? That's not as simple as we humans think it is. Cars were designed for the human body, not a canine's body.

From your dog's perspective, riding in the car doesn't make sense. The first step of riding in a car is getting into the car. Stop and think about how your dog gets into the car. When you open your car door, how can your dog get inside the car? Jump in, you think. But, how? Where? Unless your dog is getting into the bark of an SUV, with the seats folded down, there isn't a clear path into the car. First, when most car doors are open, the door is at an angle. Your dog needs to maneuver and jump into the car at an angle. That's not a typical movement for a dog. Second, many dogs don't have the strength in their back end to jump onto the seat of the car from the ground. They may put their front paws on the seat, but then their back feet slip on the car door frame while trying to scramble into the seat. That can be scary, which can prevent your dog from wanting to get into the car. Using a sturdy step and then teaching your dog how to use the step to get into the car, is a simple solution that your dog will appreciate.

Once inside the car, your dog can look out the window and see the changes in scenery, but the senses (odor and sight) are out of sync with the movement of the car. How odd it must be for a dog whose nose is the primary way to get information about the world. Driving with the window cracked just a bit changes the experience. How do dogs experience the odor filling their nostrils with the scenery passing by? Is it overwhelming or awesome, or somewhere in between?

When you're driving, you know when you need to slow

down, stop, or accelerate. You can prepare yourself physically for the change in movement. Most other human passengers in your car can anticipate the movement of your car and adjust their bodies accordingly. Your dog cannot. He has no idea when you're going to accelerate, stop, take a curve in the road, or turn a corner. He can't anticipate how to prepare for a change in direction or speed. That can keep arousal levels a bit higher, and it could put your dog on edge. How many dogs experience some sort of motion distress, and we're just not aware of it? Riding in the back seat of a car always makes me a bit queasy. Why would it be different for my dog?

When I get in the car, I know my destination: grocery store, client home, bookstore, doctor's office. When my dog gets in the car, she has no idea where we're going. It could be the veterinarian, the park, a Sniffspot, or the training facility. I often have a choice about where I go. She doesn't. If a trip in the car makes her stomach queasy, and the destination is unknown, should it surprise me that she's not excited about a car ride?

I've had a number of foster dogs who didn't enjoy car rides. I'll never know if they associated the car with being relinquished (abandoned, from their perspective) or if they never liked riding in the car. Other foster dogs loved it. One very special foster, Bam Bam, loved flying down the freeway with his head hanging out the car window. He was one of the most adaptable dogs I've ever had the pleasure of fostering. The day he was adopted, his new owner opened the back of the car, and Bam Bam hopped in, poked his head out the window, and was ready to go. No hesitation. That boy loved car rides.

Ursa was a very different story. She didn't like getting into the car until she was 18 months old. She would shake, tuck her tail, and drool once inside. I'm not sure how many hours we spent working on getting in the car. Not driving; just getting in the car. Once she was in the car and calmer (no drooling, no shaking, would take a treat), we started working on being in the car with the doors closed and windows open. And then we added being in the car, doors closed, windows open, and starting the car engine. Now she hops right in the car, puts her head out the window, and seems to enjoy car rides as long as the trips are short, and the windows are down. That does mean that even when the temperature is below freezing, and Ursa is in the car, the windows are down (at least partially). A small inconvenience that makes car trips better for her.

Creating a good home for you and your dog considers both species' needs. Your dog has species-specific needs that are different from yours. Recognizing that and making accommodations for those needs to be met decreases many of the undesirable behaviors that cause frustration for people. Meeting the needs of your dog decreases tension between you and your dog. A good home is one where everyone, regardless of species, is loved, is respected, and has appropriate accommodations made for who they are as unique individuals.

2

WHAT DOES MY DOG NEED
TO BE OKAY?

Dog owners often ask me what kind of toys are indestructible (the answer is: none), or what the best food for a dog is, or if I have a vet recommendation, or what doggy day care I recommend. Those are good questions. But it leaves out an important question. It's a question that dog owners don't ask often. What does my dog need to be okay? What is okay?

The Five Provisions of Well-Being provide a framework to ensure that our dogs live the most fulfilled lives possible. It helps us make sure that our dogs are okay, that they are living fulfilled lives. The provisions are nutrition, health, enrichment, positive mental experiences, and species-appropriate behavior.

We're living at a time when questions about the welfare of our companion pets are being reconsidered. Moving beyond simply providing food and shelter, animal welfare experts are asking questions about quality of life. The goal is providing opportunities for companion pets to live satisfying and worthwhile lives. We're trying to think from the companion animals' perspective. To do that, pet owners can provide an environment where all five provisions are met consistently. Keep in mind that to meet this challenge, we need to consider the natural behavior of our dogs, not what we, as humans, find acceptable.

Throughout our dogs' lives, adjustments need to be made to meet their needs. Most people realize that the needs of a puppy change. An 8-week-old puppy has different needs than a 6-month-old puppy. Many people don't realize that the needs of senior dogs (dogs 7 or 8 years and older) are different than those of a 2- or 3-year-old dog. While my 14-year-old dog still needs physical exercise every day, what we do has changed. Our walks are slower (really slow on some days), he needs help going up the stairs, and his fitness routine has changed to be easier on his joints. Walking our 3-year-old dog with our 14-year-old dog presents me with challenges. The younger dog can do longer, more strenuous walks. Some days, we all walk together, which means Ursa must walk a little slower than she'd prefer. On those days, Ursa gets to do a lot of find-it games, so she doesn't get frustrated. On the days Roadie is not interested in a walk, Ursa and I do more challenging walks while Roadie does less demanding exercises in the house. Our next puppy will start out doing very short walks several times a day until he or she is ready to do longer excursions. But by that time, Ursa may be a senior who is slowing down. The point is that dogs' needs change over the course of their life. As their guardians, we need to recognize the changes and adapt as needed.

Now, let's look more closely at The Five Provisions of Well-Being, beginning with nutrition. We'll take a closer look at each of the provisions and how to implement them into your dog's life.

NUTRITION . . . (LIVING OUR BEST LIFE ONE NIBBLE AT A TIME)

Food. I love food. My dogs love food. I share food with my dogs. I use food as part of training. My motto is cookies (aka, any kind of delicious treat for your dog) for everyone! That last statement might be a little over the top, but I think you get my meaning: food is valuable. It's necessary for life. Without it, we die. Too much of it, and we become diseased and die too soon. The same is true for our dogs.

Food is complex. In my mind, I separate food and nutrition. Nutrition is what my dog and I need for good health. Food brings the ideas of emotion, community, and love to my mind. Love toward family, which includes the furry beasts snoring on my couch. Yes, when I'm feeling especially affectionate toward my dogs, I'm likely to give cookies as a show of love and devotion. I have no idea if my dogs receive the extra cookies as a sign of affection, but I do know they enjoy getting those "I love you" cookies.

Nutrition seems like it should be a straightforward thing. For good health, dogs need certain nutrients: protein, fat, and carbohydrates, plus micronutrients: fatty acids, amino acids, and vitamins. Calories coming in need to be roughly equal to calories expended to maintain weight, barring a medical condition. Those are the very basics of nutrition. So why is it so complicated? That sends us back to food, which, as it turns out, brings out strong feelings and opinions among people.

Dogs are individuals with unique physiology. Just like people, what works for me may not work for you. What works for my dog may not work for your dog. Good nutrition is the foundation for good health now and as your pet ages. There are many different ways to feed your dog: kibble, freeze-dried, cooked (commercial or home-prepared), and raw (commercial or home-prepared). Over the years, I have used all of those methods to feed my dogs. In my opinion, one option is not inherently better than any other.

The needs of the individual dog and the amount of time you have to prepare balanced meals need to be considered. Just imagine preparing balanced home-cooked meals for three Great Danes and a German Shepherd. Hours of research, talking with my vet, then sourcing raw ingredients. Time-consuming? Yes! Did my dogs love it? Yes! Was that sustainable? Not for me. Personally, home-prepared food limited the amount of time I could spend *with* my dogs. I'll confess I believe their well-being suffered while I was in the kitchen. That said, when I've had elderly or sick dogs, I'm right back in the kitchen cooking for them if they need it.

The important takeaway is that how you choose to feed your dog is a discussion between you, your veterinarian, and, if you choose, your veterinary nutritionist. But it's a discussion that needs to happen. The old way of thinking – feeding your dog the same food day after day for 10 or more years – may not be the best way. When choosing how to feed your dog, you must also consider the other needs your dog has, as well as the limited time in the day that you have.

Finding good, nutritious food for your dog is a daunting task. I regularly peruse the pet store just to see what's new. And there seems to be new stuff every time I go. The pet industry is huge. It continues growing in spite of financial ups and downs. In 2022, Americans spent $136.8 billion on our pets. Food and treats accounted for $58.1 billion. Walk the aisles of any pet retailer, and you'll find many kinds of pet food and treats. You can buy food made with human-grade ingredients or organic ingredients. Need food with probiotics? Easy. Searching for limited ingredients for a sensitive stomach? No problem. Like the idea of feeding "fresh" food? Head over to the refrigerated dog food section. Now, take a moment and read the labels. Reading the labels, can you identify differences in nutritional value (protein, fat, carbohydrates, and vitamin content) of each food? You might be surprised at how similar each brand of food is to all the others. For the few dogs who have specific health issues, finding food off the shelf of your local pet store is hard. You may need a special diet that is prescribed or home prepared. But that really is a minority of the total pet dog population.

Who makes the decision about what food to get for the family dog? The dog? After all, the dog is the one eating the food. Shouldn't he have input? Typically, you choose what your dog eats. This means that pet food marketing is directed at the buyer, not the product consumer. Your dog really doesn't care what the kibble bag looks like. It's what's inside that matters. If your dog doesn't like the kibble you chose, that doesn't make him a picky eater. If I'm served food that I don't like, say pork chops, does that mean I'm a picky eater? Nope. I eat a wide variety of foods, but not pork chops. I just don't like them. If I bring a bag of kibble home that my dog doesn't eat, it may well be that she doesn't like the taste of the kibble.

Let's say that you've decided to change your dog's diet. Whom do you turn to for advice? How do you know the advice is reliable? I've read a fair amount about dog nutrition. I've taken several canine nutrition courses. I've also worked as a dog food company sales rep and in a pet store. I've lived with dogs with food allergies, kidney disease, and arthritis. I've raised puppies. My giant dogs have lived as long as 11 years when the breed average was 7 or 8 years. Should you take my advice seriously? Maybe or maybe not. I'm not a canine nutritionist, and I'm not a veterinarian, but I'm well-read on the subject. I've purchased food for my dogs based on my personal bias (human grade, freeze-dried, or oven baked, blah, blah,

blah) only to have my dogs say, "Ewww, I'd rather not eat that, thank you very much" and walk away from their morning meal. If you want solid nutritional advice, talk to a canine nutritionist. If you want to get more information about dog food from an independent third party, check out www.TheDogFoodAdvisor.com. They present "just the facts" about the nutrient content of many different brands and types of dog foods. If you need advice about food because your dog has a medical issue, talk to your veterinarian or canine nutritionist.

Choosing food for your dog shouldn't be difficult. Here are my simple guidelines for choosing food for your dog. You need to find the balance between meeting their basic nutritional needs. Look for food that meets AAFCO standards – the bag, box, or can will indicate if it's a balanced and complete meal. Once you do, you can feel sure your dog's basic nutrient needs are met. Then, you need to look at your budget. There are nutritious foods that fit almost any budget. Finally, find a food that your dog likes. Your dog really should have some say in what she eats.

HEALTH AND FITNESS . . . (DOES MY DOG NEED A GYM MEMBERSHIP?)

Maintaining good health includes routine medical care, including yearly wellness exams, immunizations, blood work, and parasite prevention. Puppies visit the vet more often during their first year, primarily for immunizations. As pets age, vet visits to manage health changes related to aging often increase. Beyond that, your vet can advise you about the frequency of vet visits for your dog.

When should you see your vet? Whenever you see a behavior change in your dog! My big, floppy-eared dog just spent several moments shaking her head. Then she sat and scratched at her ear. Then she shook her head again. While dogs do shake their heads *and* they do scratch their ears, as I watched her, I noticed that it was different: she was more focused, and the head shaking lasted longer than normal. Something about her ear was bothering her. In my mind, I went through the possibilities – dirty ear, tick or bug in her ear, ear infection, yeast infection? I practice looking into my dog's ears. It took a while for Ursa, in particular, to be relaxed about me peering into her ears. The work paid off.

I called her to me, rubbed her ears, noting any change in ear temperature, then told her, "Ear" – my cue for "I'm lifting your ear and looking inside." She let me. Her ear was a normal color, with no redness. I didn't see any bugs or foreign objects. I smelled her ear – didn't smell unusual. But I did notice a little waxy dirt. Quick ear cleaning, and she seemed fine. For the next several days, I watched her. If the ear was still troubling her tomorrow, I'd give the vet a call. Over an itchy ear? Yep. Let me explain why.

Pain and illness affect behavior in people. We know that through experience. The last time you were sick or had a headache, were you a little grumpier, or did you tend to be snappy at the people close to you? I know I'm not my normal self when I'm in pain or sick. I just want to be left alone. I don't even want people to talk to me! As it turns out, when dogs are sick or in pain, they get grumpy, too. A grumpy dog is more likely to display undesirable behavior (undesirable by human standards), such as growling, hiding, fighting, and biting.

Illness in dogs may be easier to diagnose than pain in dogs. Symptoms of illness may be obvious. Pain is different. Pain is subjective. Every individual experiences pain differently, and this is true of our dogs, too. One challenge in diagnosing pain is that dogs tend to mask pain. It's in their best interest to do so. Hiding pain prevents attack by predators, who look for the weakest animal to prey on. Why? Slow-moving animals are easier to catch and overcome. But, you say, your dog isn't living in the wild and doesn't have to worry about predators. True. But living in a home with people does not change the fact that your dog is a dog. Your dog experiences life through his doggie lens, which means that masking pain and illness is the safest thing to do.

A dog who is in pain will behave in a manner to protect themselves from feeling more pain. Wouldn't you do the same? Dozens of dogs have shared my home, both family dogs and foster dogs. One adolescent dog I fostered was gentle and well-mannered. She didn't bark or pester the kids or dogs. She walked well on a leash. Great dog, you think. Not so fast. When she was just a year old, she was diagnosed with glaucoma and became blind. The veterinary ophthalmologist told me at her initial exam that she was in constant pain, like living with a continuous migraine headache. The vet recommended removing her eyes. The rescue agreed, and we moved forward with having her eyes removed and her eyelids sewn shut. Halfway through her recovery, she started to play. She barked. She chewed a shoe. I was elated! She was acting like a normal adolescent dog! That seemingly "good" behavior was her response to pain. Doing normal doggie things, like playing, zooming, and digging, was painful. Good behavior doesn't necessarily mean your dog is feeling good. The difference between living in constant pain and living pain-free was night and day.

Sadly, not all dogs are diagnosed with painful conditions before something bad happens. Of the aggression cases I work on, many of the dogs have a medical issue. Most often, it's pain related. I'll share two instances of aggression related to medical problems in my own home. The first happened before I was a professional trainer.

Darla was one of the first dogs I ever fostered. When I picked her up from her owner, he told me she was a terrible dog. She couldn't learn anything. She was too stupid to walk on a leash. Oh, and she hated men.

Darla was a 3-year-old 180-pound brindle, Great Dane. Her fur was rough and oily. She had pressure sores on her elbows. She was frightened of the world around her. She loved other dogs. She was definitely afraid of men.

We went for her first-ever vet exam. Bloodwork revealed that she had hyperthyroidism, easily treatable with life-long medication. Once she was on the meds, her fur got soft and shiny. She lost some weight (down to 165 pounds – just right for her!). Over time, she gained confidence, learned to walk on a leash, and even discovered that the men in our home were actually pretty nice. During that first 6 months, she got LOTS of hotdogs from the guys.

Darla joined our family. She is one of only three "foster fails" out of dozens of fosters who lived in our home. She helped us welcome many more foster dogs. She greeted the neighborhood kids when they came over to play. She became the nanny dog to our first grandchild. And then she bit a child.

It happened right in front of me. No one was at fault – the kids were ignoring her. She knew the child she bit. The kids were playing catch with a ball. The child was 10 years old. When she caught the ball, Darla rushed over and bit her arm. When I called her, Darla immediately came to me. We put her in her crate and then tended to the bite wound. There were two punctures (today, I would label that a Level 3 bite). It was a very uncomfortable phone call to the girl's parents. Then I called my vet.

Why did I call my vet? Honestly, I don't know. At the time, I knew that what Darla did was not normal for her. Not normal meant I needed to call the vet. The vet was wonderful. She recognized the change and that it was outside of Darla's norm. We did bloodwork and x-rays to check for any changes. Darla's chest was full of tumors. I didn't know she was sick. She was in pain. I felt like I let her down. If only I'd realized she was . . . but I didn't. And she bit. And all our hearts were broken. Yes, I still cry for my big, goofy girl. A brief pause before I go on. Excuse me.

The next story is just as hard, or perhaps harder. Years later, we decided to get a puppy. We brought our Moonie girl home when she was 10 weeks old. She was a little blue-brindle, Great Dane. Occasionally, Moonie would limp a little for a day, then the next day, she would be fine. We thought it was growing pains or that she might develop HOD (hypertrophic osteodystrophy), so I watched her closely. I'd had a foster puppy with HOD years earlier and knew what to look for. She never developed HOD, but sometimes she would be "gimpy." Moonie went to puppy classes, lived with three other dogs, and did humane education presentations with me. I hoped she would be my working dog. And then we brought another puppy home (yes, another Great Dane).

Moonie and Ursa seemed to do well together. They ate carrots on the floor together. They played tug. They slept together. One day, Moonie attacked Ursa: one minor puncture but no serious injury. We tended to Ursa, checked out Moonie, and then called my vet. As a professional trainer and behavior consultant, I knew something was wrong and suspected we had a medical issue.

I've had the great fortune to have wonderful, compassionate veterinarians over the years. The vet drew blood and then did a thorough physical exam. She suggested doing X-rays. We were both surprised at what the X-rays revealed. Moonie was not yet 2 years old. She was at a healthy weight. We walked daily and did physical fitness work. She had a nutritious diet. But Moonie had arthritis in her spine, neck to tail. She was in pain. It made sense now. Our other dogs were older and less rowdy during play. Ursa was almost 100 pounds and loved to body slam. Of course, it would hurt Moonie! Defending herself from a rambunctious puppy was reasonable, but the intensity of the defensive behavior was surprising. Moonie had many problems and was with us only a short time before she crossed the Rainbow Bridge.

These are extreme examples. Many dogs who are in pain or have an illness will try to avoid situations that cause discomfort. My 14-year-old bully mix typically hides or tries to stay close to people when we have adolescent dog visitors. Why? He has osteoarthritis in his back and legs. He's unstable and unable to get out of the way of rambunctious play. When he's bumped into, it hurts. Yes, he does have a pain management protocol, but that won't prevent suffering when a 50-pound adolescent dog slams into him accidentally!

The veterinary community is just now starting to understand the connection between behavior changes and pain/disease. There was a time when even giving pain medication after neuters was not standard protocol. Things have changed for the better. If you see any behavior change in your dog, take her to your vet. Get a thorough exam.

Going to the vet is not a regular event for most pets, which means their behavior will be different. Your dog will feel stress at the vet's office, which will change her behavior. Your dog may show lameness at home, but at the vet, she's just fine! It's very frustrating for the owner and veterinarian.

So often, I arrive at a client's home and notice things like a stiff gait, a slight limp in a back leg, a knee twist when walking, or a shoulder being favored, and suggest a vet visit. These things affect behavior. The client goes off to the vet, and the vet finds nothing wrong. The client will tell me that the dog was absolutely fine at the vet. I don't doubt them. Dogs mask pain. Of course, they won't show pain when they are stressed at the vet. So, what's a person to do? Take videos of the changes you're seeing and show them to your vet. Ask your trainer, friend, or partner to take a video of your dog. When your dog feels safe, they are more likely to display physical discomfort.

Some of my clients have been able to find veterinarians who do house calls. One client went to their primary vet three times at my request. When I met the dog, he displayed symptoms of discomfort: his back was slightly arched (roached), one back leg was stiff when he walked, and he would flinch if approached on that side. The dog had a bite history. I suspected that part of the problem might have been related to pain. The primary vet never found a physical problem, and my client said the dog acted fine during the exams. I'm sure the vet must have thought I was crazy.

I suggested a vet who would do a house visit. My clients set up an appointment. The visiting vet was able to see the dog in his home, where he was comfortable, and sure enough, the dog acted like his usual self – roached back, stiff hind leg, and flinching when the vet did the physical exam. The vet prescribed a pain management regimen, laser treatment, and physical therapy. Once the dog's medical needs were met, we could move forward with behavior modification and training. Not every behavior change is rooted in a medical condition, but if it is, addressing it is the first step toward behavior change.

It's extremely important to partner with your veterinarian. The veterinarian's job is challenging. Think about it. They walk into an exam room and immediately have two individuals to communicate with: one speaks their language, and the other doesn't. Veterinarians often work with multiple species. Every species communicates differently. Communication alone is a constant challenge. On top of that, most animals cannot verbally tell the vet what they're feeling. And most animals, when feeling pain or disease, may become more agitated and more likely to display aggressive-type behavior when they are at the vet office being examined. That makes them generally more dangerous to work with. The painful dog isn't a bad dog. He's just trying to protect himself from further discomfort.

Even during a routine wellness exam, pets feel stress. Stress changes behavior. Your vet may see a very different animal in the office than what you see at home. One way you can help your vet and your dog is through information gathering. I have notes on my phone for my dogs. If my dog skips a meal, I make a note of it. If I see my dog limping, I make a note. Most of the time, these events are singular. But, in the case that my dog skips several meals in a week, then I know something is wrong, and I can look for other potential causes (like too many treats or chews). If I can't find a cause for the meal skipping, then a vet visit is in order. If I can tell my vet the number of meals skipped and any other changes in behavior during that time, that gives my vet valuable information that may help with diagnosis. Routine veterinary care is foundational for good health. But it's just one part. Physical fitness promotes good health.

Meeting your dog's physical needs seems straightforward: a 30-minute walk every day. Simple. Unless you have a puppy. Or a fearful dog. Or a senior dog with health issues. Or a dog recovering from surgery. Or a high-energy working dog. Or it's below zero outside. Or it's 100 degrees outside. Or you have the flu. Or it's been a very long day, and you're exhausted. It can get complicated.

There was a magical time when I walked all four of my dogs together: three Great Danes and my bully mix. I've got two dogs now and walk them separately. My bully mix is an older gentleman. He cannot physically handle a 30-minute walk. We don't get far during our short 15–20 minute walks. I have to keep a close eye on him to prevent him from overdoing it on the trail so he can get himself back to the house. It's simply not possible for me to carry a 70-pound dog. When I walk with my 3-year-old Great Dane, I know that 30 minutes is not enough on some days. Our walks are varied and rigorous. We climb over fallen trees, she zooms under logs and around trees, and we play hide-and-seek. Her stamina has increased significantly now that we incorporate more parkour and play into the walk.

A couple of years ago, I learned about dogs and parkour. I don't know how I missed it! Parkour is a great activity where you and your dog interact with objects outdoors. The basic or novice skills teach dogs to go over, around, through, and under obstacles found in the environment. When you start looking for obstacles, you'll start seeing them everywhere! Once Ursa learned these skills, our outdoor times turned into adventures. When we're on a walk, Ursa and I look at something like a fallen log as a fun obstacle: something to jump on, go over, or possibly go under. I credit doing parkour with building her confidence, increasing her overall fitness, and building our partnership. This means 30 minutes probably isn't quite enough for her now. When she was a young puppy, we'd do several 10-minute walks. Over time, the duration of the walks increased. When she's a senior, the duration will decrease. Meeting your dog's physical exercise needs will change throughout the course of their life.

Walking isn't the only way to meet your dog's fitness needs. In fact, it might not be the best way for you and your dog. There may be times when you cannot walk your dog. Walking is limited when a dog is recovering from an injury, illness, or surgery. Walking with your dog will be limited if *you* are recovering from an injury, illness, or surgery. Perhaps where you live is not safe for walking, and there are days you just can't make it to a park. Or the weather may not be safe to be out in. If it's icy, I will not take my dogs walking. The risk of injury to me or them is too great. So, what are some other options?

OUTDOOR EXERCISE

On those days when your regular walk is out of the question, or if your dog doesn't like leash walking, and more don't than do, consider these alternatives for daily exercise. If you're in an area with trees and it's safe to have your dog off-leash, hide-and-seek is a great option. It's simple: walk around with your dog. When your dog stops to sniff, duck behind a tree. It's fine if the tree doesn't completely hide you. Pause and count to three, then say, "Where am I?" using a tone of voice that invites fun. Then watch your dog. When Ursa and I do this, she lifts her head and starts looking around. If she can't see me, then she starts sniffing the air. When she's identified where she thinks I am, she gallops to me. I love watching that "aha" moment when she finds me.

Chase games are fun but not recommended for kids and dogs. Once I learned how much fun it is to chase and be chased by my dog, I've done it with all my dogs. I usually invite Ursa to chase me first. A quick tap on her side or butt, then I call, "Come and get me!" Once she gets me, I turn and say, "I'm gonna get you!" then I chase her. This is a short game. I don't want her to get over-excited and knock me down, so I limit it to just a few turns, and then I say, "All done," which means that the game is over.

The classic games of fetching the ball or catching a Frisbee are excellent exercise games to play. Some dogs love running through sprinklers. These activities count as exercise and, in many cases, are more enjoyable than leash walking.

INDOOR EXERCISE

Playing hide-and-seek indoors can be great fun. You slip out of sight, then call your dog. When they "find" you, it's a thrill for both of you. Start with easy spots, then work up to more difficult hiding spots. This is a great game for improving recall and paying attention to you. I've noticed that when I play hide-and-seek several days in a row, Ursa pays more attention to where I am, both indoors and out.

We play a game called "follow me." If I say, "Ursa, follow me," that's her cue to literally follow me wherever I'm going. It started as a safety cue. When she would get too engrossed in something, maybe sniffing something when I was ready to move on or tracking the movements of another dog, in my happiest, chirpiest voice, I'd call "Follow me!" as I made a tight U-turn and went the other way. What started as a necessary cue has become one of our favorite games. Cold and icy? Hot and humid? A few minutes of "follow me" helps my dogs get exercise indoors while building our relationship.

Indoor parkour and obstacle courses are another fun way to exercise when going outside isn't practical. This is the time to look at your environment and get creative. One cold day, Ursa and I ended up practicing parkour skills in the bathroom. I was recovering from a knee injury and hadn't walked the dogs in several days. She was restless, following me around the house, getting in my way. Anyone living with a restless dog can picture that. While I was washing my hands in the bathroom, Ursa stood staring at me. Usually, I would have been getting her dressed for our walk at that time. But no walk that day.

Then she nudged me. Then she stared at me. She was trying her best to engage with me. I sighed. My knee hurt, and I wasn't feeling particularly interested in doing anything but putting ice on it. I also knew I wasn't meeting her needs.

What to do? My go-to indoor fun things were not an option. We'd been working on parkour skills on our walks: over, under, around, paws up, get in. We'd been doing some parkour in the house, but I hadn't found anything that she could get in. She's too big for most of the boxes that are delivered. Light bulb moment: she could get "in" the bathtub! Your dog may fit in the bathtub, but Ursa barely fits. I can't bathe her in the tub, but she could jump in. So, we spent 10 minutes doing parkour – two paws on the edge of the tub, jump in the tub, jump out of the tub, lie down in the tub. Turning around in the tub was the most difficult. When I said, "All done," she went and took her normal post-walk nap.

When you look at your home through your dog's eyes, you'll find many interesting ways to have fun with your dog. If you put the kitchen table chairs in a line, your dog can weave through them. We practice "two paws" up on the kitchen chairs. For smaller dogs, teaching an army crawl under the chairs is fun. Line up the kitchen chairs or bar stools, and you have a tunnel for dogs to crawl through. Using two chairs, your dog can do figure eights around the chairs. With a single chair, you can teach your dog to "go around." The possibilities are endless.

AN ENRICHED LIFESTYLE . . . (CRITICAL THINKING INCREASES CALM BEHAVIOR)

Pop quiz time! True or false? Puzzle toys, slow feeders, and interactive toys meet your dog's need for enrichment.

Before we can answer that question, we need to understand what we mean by enrichment. Think of enrichment as providing ways for your dog to do doggie things, to express his innate behaviors. This will vary from dog to dog, but in general, enrichment activities give your dog the opportunity to dig, forage, sniff, chew or taste, and observe. I would argue that allowing a dog to bark could be included in this list. Enrichment can be active or restful. Note that some of these activities people may consider a nuisance, like digging or barking. Why does your dog need to do those things? Dogs are dogs and need opportunities to be dogs. Enrichment improves the quality of life, meeting species-specific social and mental needs. Think about ways to include physical movement, sensory experiences, food play, and cognitive games. Without enrichment, quality of life decreases. This is true for both people and pets. When done thoughtfully, enrichment can meet both your and your dog's needs.

The answer to the pop quiz above: it depends. Using toys can be part of regular enrichment, but toys may not be as beneficial as we think. If you're looking at dog toys and trying to find something to keep your dog busy, a puzzle might be a good option for some dogs, but not all dogs. If an interactive toy is frustrating your dog, she will walk away. Or if the toy is too easy for her, she may be energized but not tired. Before purchasing interactive toys that you think look fun, observe your dog. What does she do for fun? Often, the very things she finds fun are the things you don't want her doing, like digging in the trash or chewing on a rug. Using an interactive toy or activity might satisfy her urge to dig or chew. But it might not. The most efficient way to prevent unwanted chewing or digging is to provide opportunities for your dog to dig or chew.

Enrichment indoors is good. Enrichment outside, for most dogs, is great! There are exceptions to this. Dogs who are fearful may not find an outdoor adventure satisfying. When we're out for an adventure with our dogs, it can be a powerful experience. Ursa and I have a favorite SniffSpot a few minutes from our home. It's a private, almost 50-acre wooded wonderland. We can meander through paths, hills, and meadows together. Ursa and I are challenged during our 45-minute adventures. We get a more strenuous walk than our daily walks. The hills are steep in some areas. The terrain is challenging. Ursa is free to sniff, explore, or pause to observe at her leisure. Usually, she gets to the top of the hills before I do (one of the advantages of having four legs instead of two!), and she'll pause, looking back at me, waiting for me to catch up. Once I reach the top of the hill, she's ready to move on. We're experiencing the walk from each of our species-specific perspectives, but at the same time, we're experiencing the walk together.

Our outdoor adventures allow Ursa and me the opportunity to engage our senses of smell, touch, sight, and sound and to taste the world. To clarify, I am not tasting anything during our little adventures; grass and leaves do not look tasty to me. On the other hand, Ursa is a dog and not a human. A leaf, twig, or weed may look delectable to her. While she's busy tasting the flora and fauna, I often wonder what sensations she's experiencing that my human sensibilities prevent me from experiencing. Frankly, I'm probably thinking to myself, "Why does my dog do that?"

Watching Ursa sniff is fascinating. I look at the ground where her nose is buried and don't see a thing. What on earth could be so interesting? I'll never know. But she's certainly enjoying herself.

The canine nose is a wonderful thing! Many years ago, I lived with a Great Dane who was born deaf and blind. Muse was abandoned, along with her deaf brother. The story, as it was related to me, was that the puppies were left in a box at a garage sale. The lucky pups just happened to be dropped off at the home of a rescue volunteer who was having a sale at her home. Perhaps the original owners knew that the homeowner was a foster. I'll never know, but I'll always be grateful that those two pups ended up at that garage sale! From there, the foster contacted Great Dane Rescue, and the pups made their way to Great Dane Rescue foster homes.

When she was ready for adoption, I drove from Michigan to Illinois to get my little floppy eared bundle. Muse showed me new ways to experience the world. It was with Muse that I learned about nosework. Nosework is a great activity and sport for dogs and their humans (handlers). Dogs learn to search for an odor, often starting with birch essential oil or perhaps beginning with searching for food. The only cue taught is *search*. One of the things I love about this particular sport is that it's almost completely dog centered. The handler learns to observe their dog, to look for their dog's communication, and to follow their dog's nose. I credit our time doing nosework with helping her be calm and confident in the world. She learned to search methodically, trust herself, be aware of her body in her environment, and how to alert me. Muse was with us for almost 11 years. She never ceased to amaze me in all those years with her keen sense of smell and awareness of her environment. I credit Muse with teaching me the wonder and joy of the canine nose.

While I enjoy trail walking with my dogs, we don't need to leave home for an enriching activity. Dogs need time to observe the world around them. I don't think most dogs get enough time to observe their world. We spend so much time "training" the dog, "walking" the dog, "correcting" the dog . . . when do we sit and observe the world *with* the dog?

When I'm outside in the front yard, my dogs are often with me. While we do have a fenced backyard, the front yard is not fenced. Teaching the dogs to stay within the boundaries I defined is an important safety skill. While in the front yard together, I need to remain engaged with the dogs, and they need to check in with me regularly. If either dog is unable to check in or give me their attention when I call their name, then it's time to problem-solve. What is so interesting that they are unable to break away and look at me when I call their name? If it's an interesting smell, then once they've finished investigating, attention is back on me. However, if the neighbor's dog is loose and running down the street (true story) or a wild animal is taunting (oh, those squirrels), then I need to intervene. We've practiced *follow me* enough that I can usually cue *follow me,* and the dogs will follow me to the house.

It's interesting to watch how each of them interacts with the environment. Roadie sniffs around the yard, marking trees, bushes, and the perimeter. Then he finds a spot, usually in the sun, to lie down and watch. Occasionally, he'll lift his nose in the air and sniff. Once that task is complete, he heads under the steps or to a corner of one of the flower beds, digs a bit, and then lies down for a nap. After that, he generally wanders back into the house, up the stairs, and finishes napping on the couch or dog bed. This has been his pattern for about 5 years.

Ursa is very different. She watches EVERYTHING. She keeps track of me, the chickens, and Roadie. She wanders the yard, sniffs, and then checks on me. Then, she finds a good spot to lie down and observe. If I move to a new spot in the yard, she gets up, does a short patrol around me, and then goes back to her observation spot. If we get a delivery, then she stands, moves toward me, and watches the delivery person drop off the box. Then she goes back to her spot. Her wiggly excitement is a delight to see if a friend or family member drops by. She waits until the car door is open, and she sees her friend, and then she's off in a flash to greet them with wiggles, kisses, and possibly leaping in the air. Once we've gone back inside, Ursa goes off duty and naps. For Ursa and Roadie, time spent just watching the world is satisfying and enriching.

But, you say, my dog barks like crazy at everything outside!

I believe you! Ursa (and every puppy I've ever had in my home) did the same thing. Part of our routine with the puppies, adolescents, and foster dogs is spending time outside helping them acclimate to the environment. I reinforce the dogs for observing. I point out things in the environment, encouraging the dogs to look at or smell as many things as possible. The more time we spend outside in a safe space, like our yard, where the dogs can learn to observe and engage, and I can reinforce them for calm exploration, the more likely they are to remain calm when faced with something new. I encourage clients to use their yards for socialization experiences. You can teach your dog to see a dog or a person or a car and stay with you while you're in your yard. If your dog is getting too excited and needs a short break, going inside your house is easier than leaving the park. When I work with adolescent dogs who have practiced barking at people passing their yards, the very first thing we do is work on observation skills. Observing rather than reacting is my goal.

Another often overlooked lifestyle enrichment activity is what I call the shopping bag sniff fest. When I bring shopping bags into the house, it's a fun event for the dogs. Roadie sniffs the bags I set on the floor, and Ursa sniffs the bags I set on the table. That allows both dogs to sniff the bags without Roadie getting knocked over by Ursa. Bags that are set on the counter are off-limits. Anything unsafe or that is too enticing for the dogs is set on the counter. Bags that have dry goods are available for sniffing. This simple activity makes the day a little more interesting for the dogs.

Pet stores are flooded with products for enrichment. It's

easy to spend money on puzzle toys, treat balls, lick mats, and rubber toys to stuff. Keep in mind that the packaging is designed to entice you, not your dog. This may shock you, but not all dogs enjoy a Kong toy stuffed with food. Giving a dog a stuffed Kong is the go-to advice if your dog is bored, destructive, has separation anxiety, or just because you "should." I've heard owners tell me there must be something wrong with their dog because the dog wasn't interested in a stuffed Kong. Nothing wrong with the dog. The dog, like everyone else, has preferences. Enrichment is not one-size-fits-all. Enrichment is meant to provide your dog with opportunities to perform species-specific behaviors. Stuffed Kongs let the dog mimic licking and chewing marrow bones. If your dog doesn't like a Kong, maybe a marrow bone from the butcher is a better solution. Given the choice, Ursa would take a marrow bone, and Roadie prefers the stuffed Kong.

Some dogs go nuts over a lick mat. When I first introduced the lick mat, my dogs thought it was fun. Once the novelty wore off, they lost interest. They will occasionally enjoy a lick mat, but they'd rather have something else, like an empty yogurt container. I offered Ursa the choice of a peanut butter-filled lick mat or an empty peanut butter container. The lick mat had more peanut butter. She took the peanut butter container and spent half an hour licking and then tossing the container around. She had a great time! I left the lick mat on the floor just to see if anyone would enjoy it. Hours later, one of the dogs licked at it a bit, then left it alone.

My dogs' all-time favorite enrichment toy is a treat ball. I fill it with kibble and/or treats and put it on the floor. They nudge with their nose, pushing it around and following the treat trail.

It's easy to find enrichment toys that look really fun – to us. When you're shopping for enrichment toys, think about what dogs do: sniff, forage, dig, lick, shake, and shred. Toys that encourage those activities are the most likely to be engaging for your dog. If your dog can use his paw or mouth to open a trash can, drawer, or door, a more challenging puzzle-type toy could be the thing for him. The only rule of enrichment is the activity should challenge but should not frustrate the dog to the point of giving up.

POSITIVE MENTAL EXPERIENCES . . . (DO YOU CHOOSE THIS ONE OR THAT ONE?)

Did you know that 80% of dogs in the world are not owned by humans? Think about that. The vast majority of dogs are wild, village, or community dogs. These dogs are able to move about, scavenge for food, find shelter, procreate, and survive without human intervention. "Aww, poor dogs," you say. But are they? These dogs have one thing in common that many of our companion canines do not: the ability to make many choices. Some pet professionals hypothesize that the root cause of the increase in aggression and anxiety-type behaviors in the US may be the decreased agency, control, and choice in pet dogs. This makes sense to me. Have you ever heard, thought, or said any of the following statements?

- "How do I control my dog?"
- "I can't control my dog."
- "That dog needs to be controlled."
- "Your dog is out of control."

There are many products that are advertised to help you control your dog. E-collars, prong collars, and choke chains are the most common. These tools use pain to decrease or suppress behavior. What your dog is learning is that pain happens, and she associates pain with leashes, people, other dogs, or whatever other things might be in the environment. But is control over another sentient being beneficial? Control is not necessarily a positive thing. Needing to maintain control over another being is difficult. Working with our dogs' innate motivators, like allowing sniffing and digging, provides great mental and physical exercise for our dogs. A well exercised dog is generally calmer. A calm canine is what most people want.

I tell my clients that control is an illusion. I may be able to physically restrain my dog, but probably not. I'm under no illusion: I cannot physically control my dog. I know this. I accept this. So, how do I control my dog? I don't. I can't. Instead, I teach, partner, and develop trust.

Control is different than having a well-educated, well-trained dog. Training does not give you control. Training gives your dog skills to help them behave in a manner that is acceptable. Training gives you and your dog a communication system. When a guest comes to the door, what is the expectation for your dog's response? Does your dog know what to do? If not, your dog will most likely act like a normal dog: barking, bouncing, pouncing, jumping, spinning. And you may act like a person who believes they should have control of their dog – collar grabbing, pulling, yelling. In this situation, no one wins. Frankly, door greetings are extremely difficult. Management, in my opinion, is often more efficient in this situation.

The need to control every aspect of a dog's short life is all-consuming. The outdated idea that any pet dog can show dominance over a human is laughable in light of the extraordinary amount of control humans have over their dogs. A captured dog simply cannot dominate its human capturer! Do a quick survey of what your dog has complete control over. Here are a few questions to consider:

- Who chooses what kind of food your dog eats?
- Who chooses what kind of toys your dog has available to play with?
- Who chooses when and where your dog goes to potty?
- Who chooses when and where your dog walks?
- Who chooses what people your dog meets?
- Who chooses what dogs your dog meets and plays with?
- Who chooses what training your dog receives?
- Who chooses when and where your dog goes in the car?
- Who chose whom: did you decide to take your dog home, or did your dog decide to go home with you?
- Who chooses when to get medical care for your dog?
- Who chooses when and where your dog sleeps at night?
- Who chooses that your dog goes to daycare?
- Who chooses to take your dog to the dog park?
- Who chooses to take the dog patio dining?
- Who chooses to take the dog on errands and then leaves the dog alone in the car?

I could go on, but I think you get the point. Our modern pet dogs have very limited choices in their lives. And this has significant consequences for person and pet. I believe the dogs who suffer the most are the dogs who have had complete autonomy over their lives and suddenly lose it. I'm not talking about stray dogs or dogs who've gotten lost or have been relinquished to a shelter or rescue. I'm talking about dogs who have no experience being owned by people. The street dog, village dog, or rural dog who is captured and then put up for adoption. These dogs are, without their consent, placed in situations they are not prepared for and that they didn't choose. These dogs suffer extreme, often toxic stress when they lose autonomy. Often, their adopters are at a loss as to why their rescued dog is fearful, shut down, anxious, or shows aggressive behavior. These dogs may have better medical care, many toys for play, and predictable meals in their adoptive (but not chosen) home, but their quality of life suffers because their emotional state is unhealthy. Nobody wins in this situation.

Pet dogs relinquished to shelters, rescues, or to different owners also deal with stress and trauma when they lose their homes. But these dogs have had experience living in a human home. They've had relationships with people. There are times when it is necessary to rehome a pet. Sometimes, the humane decision is to rehome, but that doesn't diminish the fact that the pet doesn't have a choice in the decision. One of the most important things I've learned as a pet owner and professional trainer is that *choice is critical for well-being*. Pet dogs need the opportunity every day to make choices for themselves. It can be simple: do you want to go this way on our walk, or do you want to go that way? That's a choice. Do you want to pee on that tree or that patch of grass? That's a choice. Of the 15 different toys in your toy box, which one do you choose? As much and as often as possible, let your dog make her own decisions.

APPROPRIATE SPECIES BEHAVIOR . . . (AKA YOUR DOG IS A DOG)

Why do dogs do what they do? They are dogs first and always. But we are asking them to fit into a human-centered home. Dogs speak a different language. They are motivated by different things than humans. Dogs new to living with a family, puppies, or recently adopted dogs may not understand what the expectations are. They may actually act like dogs, which may be incompatible with human assumptions about how a "good" dog behaves.

Is it unreasonable for people to want a good dog? Not at all. Your expectations may or may not be achievable by a 6-month-old puppy. Teaching your dog to meet your expectations takes time, patience, and education. If your 14-year-old dog recently passed and you have a puppy for the first time in 14 years, you're likely to be shocked. Your 14-year-old dog had years of learning and adapting to your life. She was a good dog. The new puppy is largely ignorant of your expectations as well as lacking the skills needed to be successful in your home. Adjusting your expectations will help while you're teaching the new pup what the house rules are. The training, or more accurately education, process helps your puppy (or newly adopted dog) adapt to human standards and learn where she can express her dogginess.

Dogs do doggie things. One of the doggie things they enjoy is exploration. They enjoy exploring the world. This is often a problem for the humans in their lives. Dogs don't share the same disgust for gross things that people do. The dog who happily sniffs goose poop is often pulled away from it. That's too disgusting for many of us to tolerate. Providing opportunities for your dog to explore the world, gross things and all, is necessary for your dog's well-being.

Dogs' primary way of investigating the world is sniffing. Their nose is absolutely amazing. But sniffing can become a tension point between person and pet. Imagine being out for a walk with your dog. The dog goes to sniff, but you're on a walk, no time for sniffing! From your dog's perspective, a walk is all about sniffing.

Dogs and people view the walk differently. People walk on

sidewalks in straight lines. Or we walk on well-defined (and mostly straight) paths in parks. Dogs, given the choice, generally walk in more of a wandering or zig-zag pattern. They take frequent detours, letting their nose be their guide. People get on the well-defined walkway and let their eyes be their guide. See the disconnect? Humans and canines approach the time-honored walk very differently. And it can lead to frustration for both person and pet. A little bit of compromise can go a long way in making the walk more pleasant. Without some sort of compromise, The Walk will become The Drudgery That Must Be Done Every Day Because I Have To Walk The Dog. If that's where you are, don't walk the dog. It's making you both miserable.

Teaching a dog to heel is extremely important to some dog owners. What is a heel? The dog must walk on the left side, close to the handler, his head and shoulders even with the handler's leg. It is an impressive skill, requiring the dog to be aware of his position in relation to the handler's position while moving. The dog may not leave the handler's side. It takes concentration to maintain that position. Does walking while in a heel position meet the dog's need for enrichment? In my opinion, no, it doesn't. It's a skill, an impressive one, that requires much effort to teach and maintain. But, if your dog doesn't like heeling, or you don't care if your dog heels, or perhaps you just don't have the time or interest to teach a heel, here's your pass. I've rarely seen a dog walking in a heel position who is relaxed and enjoying the walk. I've often seen dogs zig-zagging along the walk who were relaxed and enjoying the walk.

What's your goal when you're out for a walk? Is heeling important to you? That's the important question. My dog knows the "heel" cue. We use it in Rally classes. We don't use it on our walks. I'd much rather follow my dog's nose; it's way more interesting for us both. There are times when a heel is necessary for safety. When walking through a crowded or urban area, dogs who can walk in a heel position are easier to manage. And really, heeling is about managing your dog, not enjoying a walk. Whether or not you take the time needed to teach a heel is largely guided by where you and your dog walk. How successful your dog is in walking in a heel position depends on the amount of time you can devote to teaching your dog how to heel. From your dog's perspective, it's not a normal way to go for a walk.

Another doggie activity is rolling in stuff. Usually, very smelly stuff, which falls into the "Why do dogs do that?!" category. I can tolerate a lot. I don't mind dog drool, dog farts, dog burps, dog digging, dog barking, dog sniffing . . . but the dog rolling in goose poop? I draw the line there. But my dog has no idea that a line has been drawn anywhere. She thinks, "Hey, is that goose poop? What a great thing to roll in!" All I can think is, "Ewww, gross!"

Melody was an amazing dog. She and two of her litter-mates were foster dogs. Do you have any idea how cute 8-week-old Great Dane puppies are? And just imagine having three at one time. What was I thinking? I was thinking it was temporary, just until the pups were adopted. As it turned out, two were adopted and left my home, and one stayed. Melody was smart, determined, and, well, a bit bossy. She had opinions! The day she "chased" two of my adult Great Danes into a giant crate and then sat down in front of the crate, I knew she needed to stay with us. I love a determined pup! In reality, I think the adults were probably trying to take a break from the puppies. Melody simply followed them. Why the two were in the same crate, I'll never know. Nor do I understand how 320 pounds of Great Dane fit into one 54" dog crate. To my knowledge, that was the only time it ever happened. I'm glad I got a picture because it was quite a sight!

Melody helped with the myriad of foster dogs we've hosted. She was great with puppies, under-socialized dogs, and butt-headed adolescents. Melody was off-leash reliable, would willingly go places with me, and enjoyed sleeping in on the weekends. She was practically perfect. But the poop rolling made me crazy. Was that a training issue? Not in my mind. It was one of those gross doggie things that I learned to tolerate. Keeping dry dog shampoo and grooming wipes close at hand helped me keep my commitment to letting her be her best doggie self.

Dogs need more than the basics, like food, water, shelter, and medical care. Providing our dogs with opportunities to express their innate dogginess improves their quality of life. Giving our dogs ways to have meaningful experiences improves their welfare. Meeting their needs for sound nutrition, good health, daily enrichment, outlets for species-appropriate behavior, and positive mental experiences helps our dogs live their best doggie lives. And isn't that something we want for our companion dogs? But it also affects the human-canine relationship. When our dogs are living their best doggie lives, there is an added value in our lives. A fulfilled dog is calmer. They are easier to live with. They trust us. In turn, they are more willing to listen to us.

3

HOW DO I GET MY DOG TO LISTEN TO ME?... (MOTIVATION IS POWERFUL)

What motivates a dog to comply with a request or a cue? We could say that dogs live in a cost-benefit economy. The potential outcome determines every action. If the outcome seems to be beneficial, the dog will choose to do the thing. If the outcome may not be beneficial, the dog will pause, trying to determine if the thing is beneficial or not. If the outcome is not beneficial, the dog will not do the thing.

In real life, most people expect their dog to come when called (the thing the dog may or may not do). If their dog doesn't come when called, then the dog may be labeled as stubborn, stupid, or bad. I often hear people say that their dog is stubborn. That's a code word that means, "My dog doesn't comply with my demands." Is that really stubbornness? Maybe not.

People may feel bad themselves when the dog doesn't come when called. They may feel like a failure as a dog owner. I'll dispel a myth here: no dog is 100% compliant. You may have been inspired to get a particular breed of dog by a dog you saw on TV or, in a movie or read about in a book. Those dogs are working dogs, and they are trained for specific scenarios. And they get do-overs when things don't go as planned. Dogs are sentient beings. They have good days and bad days, just like people. And just like people, dogs have off days. It's ok.

But back to that coming when called. I call it a *recall*. A *recall* is important to me. It's a safety issue. And it's a fun game. I'm a lot like my dog in that way. If it's not fun, then I'm less likely to do it. If I don't see a reason to do the thing, I won't do it. My dogs are no different. How I define fun may be different from the way you define fun. The same is true for my dog – fun for her may be different than fun for me. It's up to me to discover what's fun for my dog.

Back to that *recall*. I got distracted talking about fun. Did you see that? I started talking about *recall* and wound up talking about fun. That's a distraction from the topic. People do it all the time. And so do dogs. When I call my dog, "Ursa, here," I expect my dog to do two things: 1) look toward me and 2) come to me. But what if she looks, starts moving toward me . . . and then stops to sniff part way to me? Distraction. At that moment, I have choices. I could call her again, maybe using my mom voice. I could pause a few seconds to see if she continues. I could walk away. I could grab the cookie jar and shake it. Ursa has choices, too. She can sniff. She can return to me. She can go in another direction. She can pee.

I have a goal. Ursa coming to me. She also has goals, in this case, investigating the odor. How do I align our goals and get that recall? In other words, how do I set up the scenario so that my dog returns to me? First, I need to ask what would motivate my dog to come to me.

What is motivation? It's the reason for or what persuades

you to do something. A paycheck may motivate you to go to work each day. A squirrel running across the ground may motivate your dog to chase. An interesting thing about motivation: it's not static. Many things influence what is motivating in the moment. I enjoy gardening and landscaping in my yard. I'm highly motivated to finish my work week so I can spend my days off doing things in my yard. Unless it's too hot. Or there's a foot of snow on the ground. Then, working in my garden loses its appeal. A cookie may motivate my dog to lie down. Unless she's not hungry. Or the ground is too hot. Or she needs to pee.

What would motivate your dog to come when called (or sit or lie down or any other request)? It's simple: a beneficial outcome. In other words, your dog decides based on past experience (learning), needs (biology/genetics), preferences (self), and options (environment). The cookie in your pocket may or may not be the most motivating option at that moment. Sniffing the ground could be far more motivating than returning to you right then. So, wait a few seconds and call again. Or walk away, go back inside, and ignore your dog. Being ignored can be highly motivating!

Motivation changes. Understanding that motivation fluctuates prevents me from getting too frustrated with my dog (most of the time – I am human, though). A cookie is not always the best motivation. When my dog stops wanting the cookie, the very next thing I need to ask myself is why. What's changed? Is she full? Is she bored? What? My dog can get bored? Yes. He can.

There are dogs who will do repetitive tasks, like *fetch, sit,* or *recall* over and over and over. They seem to naturally want to do anything they are asked. And they'll appear to be joyful no matter how many times you ask for a sit, a recall, or a high five.

I've had fun working with many dogs like that. They seem to live for training and doing activities with their people.

I personally have never lived with one of those dogs. I tend to gravitate toward dogs and dog breeds that really need a good reason for doing what I ask of them. I can relate – I'm the same way. I want to know why, and if there's no compelling reason for whatever it is, I won't do it. The key here is that it has to be compelling to me. Once I'm convinced about it, then I'm all in. The same is true for the dogs I live with.

Sometimes, a cookie is not a good enough reason. One of the reasons my dogs stop complying with requests is that the extrinsic motivator – the cookie – is not beneficial. One look at my dog after the third or fourth repetition of a behavior, and I know I've lost them. They are no longer finding any benefit in what we're doing. Yes, I can change the reinforcer (the "cookie" might change to chicken instead of cheese), but then I question whether she's working for pleasure or for a paycheck. Does that matter? Maybe or maybe not. But I'll get better performance and compliance if my dog is having fun doing the activity.

My goal when I'm working with my dogs is to make progress AND keep my dog engaged in the activity (or walk or whatever it is we're doing together). This is particularly important when I want to do something with my dog that my dog really doesn't see any reason to do. Ursa and I did a Rally class together. The class was for me, and she went along with it. She couldn't care less about heeling, turning, or most of the skills we were learning. She would perform, but she needed a paycheck plus a bonus. Even when working for an increased paycheck, she had her limits. She would comply with my silly request that we do a turn twice – then it was time to move on. She would heel happily, but a tucked sit in a heel position – not really her thing. If I asked for a down in a heel position – okay, but she needed overtime pay. Occasionally, we might get three repetitions, but then she was finished. What she did enjoy was spending time with me and the trainer. She enjoyed the treats. She would comply, not because she enjoyed Rally, but because it included two of her favorite things: doing something with me and getting liver. Honestly, it was probably the liver, and I just happened to be the liver dispenser.

That same dog will do parkour for an hour without any kind of treat. She'll explore the woods with me, checking in regularly whether I have cookies with me or not. Why? Those activities are intrinsically motivating. She enjoys them. Activities like parkour, sniffing, or exploring are reinforcing. When I need a recall in the woods, I can use her love of sniffing or jumping over a log as a reinforcer. In that situation, the activity is more reinforcing and more motivating than a cookie.

When I'm looking for an activity or a sport to do with my dog, one of the things I'm looking for is whether or not the dog enjoys the activity intrinsically. Does Ursa see a log and think, "Oh my gosh, it's a log, and logs are for jumping over – woo hoo, watch me fly!" or "Oh my gosh, it's a log, and jumping over the log predicts cookie." Neither is right or wrong. What I'm looking for when choosing a sport for us is the former. Love of doing the activity. I used cookies to reinforce Ursa for jumping over an agility jump with good form. Good form prevents injury. But when she discovered the fun of jumping over things, she actively looked for objects to jump over. Unlike my previous Great Danes, Ursa doesn't get overjoyed when doing nosework. She'll do it, but it seems like she's working for a paycheck rather than working for fun. But show her a log to go over or under, a tub to jump into, brush piles to go around, and she's all in. Seeing her joy in doing an activity makes training fun for me. If it's fun for me, I'm likely to train more often. Motivation is as important for me as it is for my dog.

Keep in mind that motivation changes. It changes moment by moment throughout the day. That is true for all beings. One minute, the top motivating goal may be finding food, seeking safety, or pooping. Once that need is met or the conditions in the environment change, the motivational state changes. The takeaway: dogs aren't static, and neither is what motivates them.

Motivation is critical to understanding your dog. When I call my 14-year-old bully mix to come inside, it may be a moment for me to practice patience and calm. He moves slowly, very slowly. Arthritis is taking its toll. He walks slowly. He doesn't run at all. He spends a lot of time sniffing. If I try to hurry him along, he freezes. Picture this real-life scenario: I've been working at my desk. Suddenly, I realize I need to leave the house in 10 minutes. Generally, that's not a problem. Let the dogs out, grab my bag, let the dogs back inside, and leave. I let the dogs out like normal. My older gentleman walks very slowly to the far back of the yard. Meanwhile, I've grabbed my bag, found the keys, I've got my shoes on, and I'm ready to go. He's just now found a pee spot. Now he's sniffing. I give him a happy "Roadie, come inside." He starts moving toward the house. The clock is ticking. I'm starting to get impatient. So, I do exactly the wrong thing: I call him in my "hurry up" voice. He stops moving. Then he starts sniffing. My impatience has either confused him or frightened him. While I didn't yell at him, I did speak in a lower tone of voice. For dogs, a low tone can signal danger, which will trigger avoidance behavior (freeze/sniff). My behavior changed his motivation. My impatient voice sent the message to stay away and let things calm down before going inside. Oops! Causing him concern was not my goal.

My behavior – words and body language – influences my dog's motivation. It changes his behavior. Roadie is not coming toward the house. And now I will be late leaving. Calling him again will not help. At that moment, a cookie will not motivate him. I have choices. I can put my bags down, brew a cup of tea, and wait. I can get upset. Neither of these two options does anything to change Roadie's motivational state. From past experience, I know that if Roadie is frightened, anxious, or unsure, the most beneficial thing I can do is go to him, rub his shoulders, and ask him to walk with me. To do that means I must be patient and calm myself.

It's fascinating to learn what motivates your dog and how to identify when your dog's motivational state changes. Motivational states may include satisfying physical needs (eating, drinking, peeing). The environment affects motivational states, too. Things to sniff, dirt to dig in, squirrels to chase, and things to bark at. Time of day influences motivational states as well. Some dogs are slow to get up in the morning but in the afternoon are eager for adventure. Often overlooked is the effect of pain and illness on motivation and behavior overall.

One study by Daniel Mills and colleagues demonstrated the effect of pain and illness on behavior in companion pets. It suggested that up to 80 percent of behavior problems, such as resource guarding, biting, house-soiling, attention-seeking behavior, fear, and compulsive behaviors, were associated with pain or illness. That is an astonishing number! Or is it? What may be more astonishing is that we don't connect the relationship between discomfort and change in behavior in our companion pets. When was the last time you felt pain? Headaches are common ailments. When I get a headache, my behavior changes. I'm irritable, less patient, more likely to be snappy, and my work performance decreases. It's hard to train dogs and teach people when I have a headache. Pain, illness, and disease will change your dog's motivation. While dogs are masters at hiding discomfort, that doesn't mean it's not there or that it doesn't affect how they behave.

REINFORCERS THAT MOTIVATE . . . (PAYDAY!!)

Food is a primary reinforcer. It's necessary for living. Dogs know this and respond accordingly. That's why food is often used as a reinforcer: it's highly motivating. It's more motivating than a pat on the head. But sometimes, there are other things and activities that may surpass food as a motivating factor. If your dog is full, food is less motivating. Labrador Retrievers may be an exception to this. Labs never seem to tire of food. Eleanor Raffan and colleagues identified a gene mutation that increases food motivation in some dogs. Labrador and Flat-Coated Retrievers seem to be prone to this mutation. If you think your Labrador is always obsessed with food, you're not imaging it.

But, you say, I don't want to use food. Isn't praising my dog good enough? I occasionally hear that from people. My question is this: "Would you do what your boss asks for verbal praise, or do you expect to be paid for working?" Money is a strong reinforcer for humans. Another challenge when using words alone is that your dog may associate your words with unpleasant consequences. If you have a history of using your words to coerce or lure your dog into situations that are frightening to your dog, then praise is unlikely to be reinforcing. An example would be coaxing your dog to greet a stranger when your dog is displaying signs of fear or concern. This decreases your dog's trust. There are other things we can use as reinforcers. We'll cover that later in the chapter. For now, we'll focus on using food as a reinforcer.

Occasionally, I'll meet a dog who is reported not to be motivated by food. This gives me pause. Why would a dog not be motivated by food? Without food, the dog will die. It's important for me to understand why a dog wouldn't want food. Is the dog overweight? Does she suffer from bouts of gas or diarrhea? Do there appear to be skin problems like excessive itchiness, dander, hot spots, loss of fur, or red skin? Is he a picky eater? This suggests a medical condition that needs to be resolved. Does he eat only when everyone is home at night? Does she only graze, never finishing an appropriate portion of food? Does she skip meals? This could signal some level of anxiety that needs to be addressed. Inappetence should be taken seriously and discussed with your veterinarian or veterinary behaviorist.

If your dog is hungry, however, they may be more difficult to train. Hungry dogs may grab food hard, have a difficult time focusing on a task, and may be highly aroused at the sight or smell of treats. I used to believe that a hungry dog was easier to train. I now know that is not true. There is a balance that each person must determine about their dog. And it changes over time as your dog develops and matures. What is true for your 2-year-old dog may be different for that same dog when she's 5 years old or 14 years old.

But let's say that your dog just isn't into food. Maybe he's overweight. Maybe she gets her caloric needs met with her meals. That checks: a full stomach will decrease the value of food. If you wanted to use food for training, the simplest thing to do is decrease the amount of kibble served at each meal. I do this for my dogs. That gives me the option of using food as a reinforcer without being concerned about my dog gaining weight. What about using kibble as a reinforcer? Sometimes, we need to for medical reasons. But, let's be honest, what's more reinforcing to you – dry toast or an omelet with a side of buttered toast? Kibble in a bowl is B-O-R-I-N-G! Your dog is fed kibble every day for their entire life. Sometimes, they are fed the same kibble – that's even more boring and not motivating.

Kibble can work for quick training sessions (1–2 minutes) at mealtime. It's a great way to practice *recall*, *attention*, and *stationing* (on a crate or mat). Kibble is not likely to work in a group class. I see it often. A person and their dog walk into a group class. They are ready – the dog is wearing a harness with a standard leash, their person has a treat pouch in hand, and they are ready to learn. And then nothing. The dog is ignoring the person. "But," the person says, "he always works for kibble at home." And I say, of course, home is a known place, he's comfortable there, and there are fewer distractions – which makes it a lower arousal place. Group class is extremely exciting. I give them a few freeze-dried treats and the dog starts working for food.

What else can be used to motivate your dog? A game of tug or fetch could be highly reinforcing. Access to sniffing or the backyard may be motivating. If you have a positive relationship with your dog and a history of reinforcing your dog, verbal praise can become motivating. Keep in mind that what may seem motivating to you may not be motivating to your dog.

Understanding what motivates the dogs in my home helps me answer the question, "Why does my dog do that?" Internal motivators, the unseen drivers of behavior, are often the most interesting and the most frustrating. Why does my dog dig? He can smell the mole underground. It's hot, and he wants to cool off. He needs to burn energy. That piece of popcorn buried in the couch is calling his name. Those are examples of internal motivation. He's acting on his own, making his own choices in accordance with innate behavior. We also need to ask ourselves what motivates our dogs to learn the skills we need them to know to be successful in life. That's where external motivators, like food or toys, become powerful. Using "paydays" to teach skills needed for happy human-dog living. The dog may be wondering, "Why do I need to sit before the kibble bowl hits the floor? It makes no sense, but it works, so I'll do it." Finally, what motivates us to teach our dogs the skills they need? For me, sharing life with my dog is the motivating factor. I want her to be part of my world. I want her to be safe. I want to explore the world together.

4

EXPLORING THE WORLD...
(SAFELY, OF COURSE)

My dog and I share something in common: we both love to explore. Knowing that about my dog, I'm more likely to be understanding when she's fully engaged in exploring her world. When she's in that state, I may not exist. The same is true when I'm exploring the local gardening center or plant shop – I might wander off, deep in thought, forgetting that my husband joined me for the shopping excursion, completely ignoring him. In a perfect world, my dog could explore safely wherever we are. In that perfect world, I could have all the plants. We don't live in a perfect world. As my dog's guardian, I need to do all I can to keep her safe. Safety is a combination of managing the environment and teaching skills to prevent injury.

There are many things that could cause potential harm in my house, such as food (onions, chocolate), furniture (jumping off onto a hard surface), and house plants (most kept out of doggie reach). There are potential hazards in my yard, including a pond (I have no idea if either of my dogs can swim), nails (months after a new roof was installed, I'm still finding roofing nails), deck and boardwalk (slippery when icy or wet), and animals (loose dogs, skunks, coyotes). Most safety is done through management. We have a physical fence, I shovel the walkways when it snows, food is kept out of doggie reach, and we have rugs on the floor to prevent the dogs from slipping on the floor. Those things are within my control.

There are skills my dogs learn that fall under the safety category, such as *recall*, *wait/go*, and *drop it*. And, of course, polite leash walking. Teaching any skill requires a significant investment of your time, but the benefits are worth it! Generally, I work on those skills that are the most difficult for my dog and the most important for my dog's safety. In my opinion, *recall* is number one for safety, followed closely by *drop it*, with *wait/go* coming in third and leash walking last on my safety list. Your list will be different needs based on your lifestyle.

Recall, coming back to me when I call, can prevent tragedy. When Ursa was having a particularly adolescent moment during a training session in our yard, she had a bout of zoomies. If a 150-pound dog goes full zoomie, then holding onto a leash is not a safe or possible option for the human! Ursa pulled the leash out of my hand and zoomed right into the street in front of our home. I was panicking. I ran to the end of our yard and, in my best happy voice, called to her: "Ursa, here!" And she did, which earned her a reinforcer. But she ran into the street. Why did I give her a reinforcer? Because she performed a lovely recall. She did exactly what I asked her to do. My heart was racing. Pretty sure I developed a few more gray hairs, but she did return. During her bout of zoomies, she was mentally in a different world. Getting angry with her for zooming would not have benefited either of us. It might have prevented that wonderful recall. If I'd been angry and used an angry voice, I'm positive she would not have come back to me. Worse, she might have become frightened of the anger in my voice and kept running. Recalls are so important that I practice them daily with my dogs.

Drop it is another skill critical for safety. First, I will not chase a dog who has a shoe, sock, or child's toy in his mouth. Nor will I forcibly take something out of a dog's mouth unless it is life-threatening. Both of those human behaviors set up both person and pet for lots of frustration. Rather, I prevent my dog from gaining access to things I don't want her to have while I'm teaching her to *drop it.* Nothing in my home is more valuable than having my dog trust me. Once trust is broken, keeping my dog safe becomes much more difficult. If I leave my shoes out while I have a mouthing, teething puppy, and the puppy chews on my shoes, that's on me. It's easy to put my shoes in the closet and close the door. If my puppy chews on something that I don't want him to chew on, it's in my best interest to provide better options for him. As the human adult in the house, it's up to me to meet the needs of the dogs. They are completely reliant on me to meet all their needs. It's a heavy responsibility.

Let's go back to the issue of trust. Why is trust important? You may have had dogs for years but never thought about the need for trust. There are two primary reasons that trust is important. First, trust is critical for a good relationship. It's necessary for a strong person-pet bond. The reason I have dogs in my home is that I want to live with dogs. I want to share life together. Which means, for me, that I want my dogs to choose to spend time with me, near me, snuggling on the couch, lounging in the yard, and going for long walks. Without trust, they might avoid letting me pet them and choose to keep their distance rather than leaning on me.

There's also a practical reason for building trust between you and your dog. If your dog learns that complying with your requests results in undesirable outcomes, your dog may not listen to you. Or your dog may behave in a manner that is scary. Here's a typical example. Let's say that I bring a new puppy home. She's 10 weeks old. I'm eager to socialize her, so I take her to the local pet store. While in the pet store, several people fawn over my pup, touching her and getting close to her face. I notice she's a little reluctant, so I nudge her toward the people. Maybe I lure her with food toward the people.

We continue this for several weeks or months. The more she backs away from people, the more I "encourage" her to go meet people or for people to approach her. One day, she snaps at someone trying to pet her. I'm shocked. This is exactly what I've been trying to avoid. Why did she snap at the person? One reason is trust. My puppy learned that she could not trust me to keep her safe. She learned that it was up to her to keep herself safe, so she defended herself. She was a dog doing a doggie thing. So, what happens when I take this puppy to the vet? Her experience so far with people is that people are scary, and I won't advocate for her, nor have I prepared her to be okay with strangers. It won't be pleasant for anyone. To be crystal clear, I would never put my puppy in that situation. This is a fictitious example but one that happens all too often.

Let's say Ursa grabbed something she shouldn't have, such as a sock. If I chase her to get the sock, she just learned that grabbing a sock is the best way to engage in play. Dogs love chasing and being chased. But what if I ignore her? Or walk into the kitchen? What will she do next? If I walk into the kitchen and say, "Do you want a carrot?" I know, without question, that Ursa will walk into the kitchen and sit by the fridge. She will drop anything in her mouth for a carrot. No chasing, no sticking my hand into my dog's mouth. Knowing what is highly motivating to your dog is the key to success.

But what if Ursa caught one of the chickens? Would she drop it? The answer is yes. It has happened. When Ursa was a young adolescent, while we were teaching her to observe rather than chase the hens, we got real life (heart stopping) practice. The plan had been to spend a few minutes practicing watching the chickens. We'd been doing this for several days and had a routine. Ursa and I would head out to the coop together, and I would station Ursa on her place (yoga mat on the ground). We'd hang out, and Ursa would be reinforced for watching while being relaxed. On that particular day, when we went outside, before Ursa was on her place, Dorie (our escape artist, adventure loving hen) was foraging in the garden. Ursa noticed her well before I did. Okay, I didn't see her at all! What would you expect a 12-month-old adolescent dog to do when presented with a chicken in the garden? If you guessed chase, you'd be correct. Not only did Ursa bound away at the speed of light, but she also caught Dorie in a flash. In my happy, chirpy voice, I called Ursa to me. She trotted right over, Dorie in her mouth and not looking too happy about it. Thoughts were flying through my mind: What if she doesn't drop Dorie? Is Dorie hurt? Dead? Still using my happy voice and not expecting a positive outcome, I said, "Drop it." To my amazement, Ursa dropped Dorie, who lay on the ground very still. I scattered a huge handful of cookies on the ground, away from Dorie, and cued Ursa to *find it*. Ursa happily went off to find the cookies while I attended to Dorie. Dorie was fine, soaked in dog drool, and rather offended at having been in a dog's mouth. I scooped her up, returned her to the coop, and returned to Ursa. We finished our training session and went on with our day. For the next 2 weeks, every time we went outside, Ursa looked in the garden for Dorie. I'd love to say that Dorie gave up her exploring ways, but no. She was an explorer at heart.

I teach *drop it* when we play. Ursa brings a toy to me, asking for some playtime. We tug. I see her getting more excited, which often means grabbing the toy too hard or moving her mouth up the toy toward my hand. Before things get too wild, I'll ask her to *drop it,* then pause and resume play. That's how I prevent over-arousal when we play tug. We practice *drop it* frequently, often in the context of the play, just in case I need her to drop something that could be harmful. Our experience with Dorie makes me confident that if I did need her to drop something, she would because we practice often.

The next pair of skills is more about my safety than my dog's safety. I use *wait* and *go* in many situations. *Wait* means stop where you are. But there's also an element of anticipation because another cue is coming within a few seconds. *Go* means to move forward. I may ask one dog to *wait* at the door while I tell another dog to *go.* This prevents a mad dash out the door. Or I may ask both dogs to *wait* at the door while I go through, or have the dogs *go* through the door, then *wait* while I go out after them. On leash walks, the same cues, *wait* and *go,* help me manage the dogs and keep everyone safe. I use the same cues when getting in or out of the car.

I'm a 5-foot-tall woman. I live with very large dogs who would tower over me if they stood up on their hind legs. With few exceptions, my dogs typically weigh well over 100 pounds, usually close to 120–150 pounds. I am mindful that a dog could accidentally knock me down the stairs. The home I have now is a quirky quad-level that has three sets of steps inside. And I live on a hill, so whether I leave out the front or the back door, there are long stairways down to the ground. Anytime I'm at the top of a staircase, and a dog is behind me, I have an irrational fear that the dog will run past me and knock me down the stairs. To be honest, in the 20 years I've lived with giant dogs, this has never happened. The fear may be irrational, but it feels real.

Most often, when I'm at the top of the stairs, I'll tell the dogs to *go,* which means move forward. Once they are at the bottom of the stairs, I walk down. If someone starts to come back up, I'll ask them to *wait,* which means stop where you are. These simple skills make me feel safe.

Leash walking is complicated. It's not a single skill but rather a combination of skills that both human and canine need to learn. For now, we'll look at leash walking from a safety perspective. A number of my clients have been injured when they were dragged while walking their dogs. I have, too. Some clients have reported that their dog was attacked while on a walk by an off-leash dog or a dog running through an invisible fence. I, too, have had a dog attacked by an off-leash dog during a walk. Dog fights can happen when dogs meet on leash. These are serious problems that don't have simple answers.

When we are out with our dogs, much of the environment is out of our control. Dogs can get paw injuries walking on hot or cold sidewalks. Paws can be injured by glass or thorns while out on a walk. Dogs may be frightened by people rushing up to greet them. (Please don't do this! There really is no reason to engage with a stranger's dog. It's rude. It puts the dog in a terrible situation. Admire the dog from a distance – it's the safest and most respectful way to interact with an unknown dog.) In short, leash walking is complicated.

But don't dogs need to be leash-walked every day for 30 minutes? Possibly, but it depends. If your dog is an anxious wreck, who's afraid while on that 30-minute walk, I'd say no. The leash walk is doing more harm than good. If you can find a place where you and your dog feel safe, then a walk can be beneficial. Personally, I've had enough negative experiences with people and dogs while walking my dogs that I no longer walk my dogs in public parks or in town. We walk only on private property. I feel safer, which means I'm more relaxed. If I'm relaxed, so are they. Our walks are pleasant. After a walk, I feel rejuvenated, and my dogs are calm and happy. Going for pleasant walks is good exercise, but don't limit your dog's exercise to a daily walk.

When we consider safety, there are two perspectives: ours and our dogs. I may be convinced that what my dog is doing is dangerous. My dog may think it is perfectly normal and feel calm and confident. What I may believe is safe, my dogs may consider terrifying or at least concerning. Who's right? It depends. In addition to considering perceptions of safety, there are adjustments we make to our dog's environment for safety, and then there are skills that we teach for safety.

During our walks, Roadie is off-leash; Ursa wears a harness, sometimes with a leash and sometimes off-leash. There are turkey, coyote, fox, deer, and other woodland critters that inhabit the woods. This means there is a variety of pee, poop, and on occasion, dead animal. Occasionally, we'll find old fencing, landscaping timbers, golf balls, and tires on the property left behind by previous owners. We follow trails for most of the walk but also spend a fair amount of time off-trail. This lets us practice parkour skills: on, off, over, under, through, in, out, around, and wait. While the woods are a great place for us to walk, they're full of potential hazards.

Let's look at the above scenario from a safety perspective. First, to leash or not to leash: what's the best option? It depends. Roadie is off-leash reliable. That wasn't always the case, but now I'm confident he won't wander too far away or get lost. When he gets scared, he freezes or finds me. Ursa is different. She still gets zoomies, although less often. In those bursts of energy, she's less likely to return to me. She is on leash during walks for another more serious reason: when she gets scared, she runs. I can't always predict what will frighten her. I'd much rather be safe and let her wear a leash than lose her.

Another reason for the leash and harness is Ursa loves doing parkour. Since she wears a harness, it's easy for me to spot her when she's trying something new or to prevent her from falling when she gets a little overconfident or a log is slippery. Preventing injury is always on my mind!

Left-behind rubbish – fencing, landscaping material, golf balls, broken bottles, and other stuff – is never fun to find. When I see junk like this, I move my dogs away with a directional cue, like *this way* or *with me*. Again, preventing injury is a big deal to me, and these things are potential hazards. Better to explore other things.

But how do my dogs experience this environment? While I'm on the lookout for potential hazards, hopefully, my dogs are just being dogs. That's why we're in the woods! This is where I need to be particularly cognizant of the fact that my dogs are not humans. What they find delightful sometimes makes my stomach turn. When Ursa finds a carcass, she'll want to sniff. Other dogs might want to roll in it. Gross but normal. She sees nothing disgusting about it. If I didn't let her sniff the carcass, I would be denying her the opportunity to be a dog, which is the reason for the walk in the woods, right? Am I concerned that she would start munching on the carcass? Not really.

Why am I not concerned about snacking on a carcass? First, I know Ursa. In her early days, I gave her the opportunity to interact with weird and unusual things. Then I watched what she did, and how she interacted with new objects. Generally, she didn't put things in her mouth, so munching on a carcass would be outside of her normal behavior. Don't get me wrong. She was a typical puppy, mouthing and biting things as she learned about her world. What I am saying is that when presented with a novel item, putting it into her mouth is not her default behavior. Second, she has a long history of being reinforced for sniffing and then looking at me.

I expect dogs to be dogs, which means sniffing is an important part of how they learn about their environment. During Ursa's puppyhood and adolescence, we spent a lot of time (and I mean hours upon hours upon hours) practicing sniffing and getting reinforced for sniffing. I also spent time pointing things out to Ursa, like rocks, dirt, plants, and logs, and reinforcing her for sniffing the object. Her sniff time also included checking out the garbage can, shoes, parked cars, and any other object that she showed interest in. Anytime she sniffed, she was reinforced with ear rubs, attention, or food. Why spend so much time reinforcing sniffing if that's a normal behavior? Because I imagine my dog sniffing something amazing, like deer poop, and then possibly deciding to give it a taste. While I know poop eating is normal for dogs, it doesn't fit into my human sensibilities of what is acceptable. The challenge is: how can I provide time for my dog to be a dog while not being grossed out by that very normal doggie behavior? It seems simple – reinforce the doggie behaviors that I can live with, like sniffing. We've practiced (and continue to practice) the "sniff but don't nibble" skill enough that most of the time when Ursa is sniffing, she turns and looks at me when she's finished, expecting some kind of reinforcer. At this point, we've done this so many times I can praise her (good girl!), rub her ears, and occasionally give her a cookie. The reality is that she is still a dog, and she might go in for that nibble of something gross. As long as it isn't life-threatening, I let her have her moment. That does mean that she could eat poop, and I would let her, as gross as it might be.

Another reason I'm not too concerned that Ursa will grab the carcass is that she doesn't have a history of grabbing something, running, and having me chase her. And she will consistently drop things when cued. On the rare occasion when I might need to remove something from my dog's mouth for safety reasons, first, I'll ask her to *drop it.* If it's really urgent that I retrieve something, then, and only then, would I consider opening her mouth and retrieving an item. Ursa is 3 years old. I cannot recall a single instance where I've forcefully removed something from her mouth.

But what about sticks or non-toxic mulch? Should my dog be allowed to sniff or chew on these things? A dog holding a stick or piece of mulch is normal. It's one way a dog learns about their environment. Every time a dog is scolded for exploring their environment, the dog learns that the world is not safe. They learn that they need to be "sneaky" about displaying the species' normal behavior (dogginess). Or, over time they may learn to stop engaging with their world. Being denied the opportunity to display normal, species-specific behaviors (digging, chewing, sniffing, foraging) decreases their well-being and quality of life.

When we're out in the woods, we occasionally come across things that my dogs find fascinating but are simply not safe for them to explore, like pieces of old barbed wire fencing. Recently, Ursa and I were out hiking, and we did find, barbed wire on the ground. Her sniffing is what alerted me to it. While I'm confident that Ursa would sniff and move on, my concern was that she might step on it and get cut. In that particular instance, I cued *let's go* and moved away from the object. Ursa was willing to miss out on the sniffing opportunity because she knew she would have other chances to sniff. Her experience and history of reinforcement for "legal" sniffing helped her forego the unsafe sniff spot.

Exploring the world together is one of the greatest benefits of having a dog. There are few things that bring me joy as much as an outdoor explore with my dogs. Outdoor adventures provide space for dogs to just be dogs. It can be great fun to observe your dog and spend time pondering, "Why does my dog do that?" Look at the outdoors as an opportunity for your dog to explore, sniff, jump over, dig, and, yes, taste their world. While keeping them safe during an explore is critical, teaching a few skills, like *drop it, wait,* and *go,* gives you the tools necessary to help keep your dog safe. A strong history of practicing those skills can prevent injury to your dog and silly chickens like Dorie.

5
DOUBLE STANDARDS...(DOGS REALLY AREN'T HUMAN)

Humans tend to be space invaders. We can't seem to help ourselves. We hug. We kiss. We cuddle. That's how we show love to other people. People have individual levels of tolerance for close encounters. I may accept or even want a hug from my partner or child, but not a stranger. A stranger coming close to me could set off alarm bells – danger! Sometimes, I don't want a hug from anyone, family and friends included. I may be feeling pain, or I may be focused on something and don't want to be disturbed. I might be asleep. Generally, other people understand and are respectful of each other's physical boundaries. Isn't it odd that people generally don't extend the same respect to other species, particularly dogs?

HOSTAGE SITUATIONS (. . . OR WAS THAT A HUG?)

Hugging is such a natural human behavior. Actually, it's a common behavior among other primates, too. It's hard to imagine not hugging. Have you ever stopped to consider what a hug is? What are the physical behaviors we engage in when we hug? Let's break it down:

1. Person A moves close – very close, within inches – of Person B
2. Person A wraps their arms around Person B
3. Person A applies pressure, pulling Person B closer
4. Person A holds Person B close to their body for some period of time

What I'm describing could be a show of affection or a hostage situation! Does Person B know Person A? Does Person B like or have any affection toward Person A? Did Person B signal that a hug would be welcome? Does Person A have bad breath?

I'm not one to show physical affection except toward people (and dogs) I know very well. As a kid, I hated visiting extended family. Being hugged by people I didn't know well or who grabbed me and wouldn't let go scared me. As a child, I really had no choice but to comply or face unpleasant consequences. So, I stood there and let the relatives hug me. From my perspective, it was like a hostage situation. I couldn't get away to safety. Did they have any idea that hugging made me feel uncomfortable? It probably never occurred to anyone in my family that a child – I or any other child – might not like being hugged. We were family, after all! Advocating for myself was not an option. In that power dynamic, the adults have all the power; the child has none.

Many people consider their pet dogs to be family members. I know I do. I also know it's very easy to forget that my canine family member is not human. Some days, I need to remind myself that my family is diverse: it's a multi-species home!

Which helps me remember that my dogs may be confused by my human behavior. Some of their species-specific behavior often confuses me, too. Many people (but not all) feel loved or comforted when they give or receive a hug. The idea that our beloved pet dogs don't like or enjoy our hugs is hard to accept. When I point out to clients how their dog's body language changes when they hug the dog, they are shocked. What does that change look like? Her body may stiffen, or sometimes there's a lip lick, her eyes widen, she shrinks back, or her head turns away. But we expect the dog to accept our hugs. That expectation can set everyone up for miscommunication and broken trust.

Hugs, from a dog's perspective, are not safe. When a human hugs a dog, the dog is stuck, trapped – she can't get away. Hugs from a human may trigger fear, which can cause a dog to try to get to safety. When hugged, a dog may look away, may push his paws into the person, may try to wriggle free. When these attempts at fleeing fail, he may stiffen, freeze, growl, and in the worst case, bite. Think about other times when a dog is "hugged" against her will. The vet may physically restrain your dog during an exam or procedure, creating an association between discomfort and being hugged. Is this intentional? Of course not, but it can happen. If your dog needs to be regularly groomed, "hugging" (physical restraint) is often part of the process and may also cause fear. From your dog's perspective, hugs may be associated with pain, discomfort, and stress. When their favorite human does something that causes her fear, it's confusing.

But, being the human that I am, I enjoy hugging my dog. Ursa tolerates it, and occasionally she'll lean into the hug, which only makes me want to hug her more. Her leaning into me is a very high-value reinforcer for me! Knowing how much I enjoy hugging my dogs, I started desensitizing Ursa to my obnoxious human behavior when she was a young puppy. This is just one of the many processes we go through to help bring harmony to our multi-species home. But I'm fully aware that hugging will never be her first choice to receive physical affection. For Ursa, and most of the Great Danes that have lived in my family, ear rubs have tended to be their top choice. I can't understand how an ear rub could be so meaningful, but I'm not a dog. Often, we do an exchange: Ursa consents to my hug, and then, I rub her ears. It's an excellent trade.

OTHER ODD, BUT SEEMINGLY HARMLESS, HUMAN-ANIMAL INTERACTIONS . . . (OR MAYBE NOT SO HARMLESS)

Head patting is just an odd thing to do. Adults do it to children, and all people seem to pat dogs on the head. What are we trying to convey with a head pat? It seems a little off-putting to me. Think about it. If something swooped down over your head, wouldn't you flinch or step away and look up to see what it was?

In my mind, I associate head patting with punishment. As a kid, being whacked on the head, even jokingly, was emotionally and sometimes physically uncomfortable. And certainly, it felt demeaning for adults to pat my head, even if they thought they were being nice.

I've had people tell me their dog was abused. When I ask about it, the most common answer is, "He flinches when I go to pat his head." Flinching is actually a normal reflex to a perceived threat. People flinch when something passes closely over their heads. Like hugging, head patting can be confusing to your dog. It can signal a potential threat, even if the dog has never been hit.

Slapping dogs on the back or side is another weird thing

that people do to animals. When people slap someone else on the back, it's often in the context of celebrating. It means, "Way to go, great job!" But if you walk up to your dog and start petting him, then start back-slapping, what are you saying? What does the dog think you're saying? One minute the human is enjoyable to the dog (assuming your dog is enjoying being petted at that moment), then the next minute, the human is whacking the dog. Would that kind of erratic behavior signal to the dog that people are unpredictable and cause pain? Possibly.

I remember being in a veterinarian's office with one of my dogs who had osteoarthritis in her back. As we waited for the vet to come in, the vet tech was petting her. My dog was calm, relaxed, and had a slow-wagging tail. All was going well. Then the vet tech started slapping my dog on her side. My dog flinched. In a split second, the vet visit went from safe to scary. I asked the vet tech to stop, and it was causing my dog discomfort. The vet tech informed me that it didn't hurt and that all dogs loved being slapped on the side.

Okay, some dogs might like being slapped on the back or sides, but they can't really tell us. Or can they? If a dog moves away, startles, flinches, turns their head, or lowers their head, perhaps they are saying, "Please stop," and we're just not listening. At that moment in the vet's office, my dog's body language said she didn't like it, please stop. Whether being slapped on the sides and back was painful or she simply didn't like it, I'll never really know. And the reason doesn't matter. What does matter is whether or not I was her advocate, her spokesperson. At that moment, we slipped out for a potty break. I needed a break, and so did my dog. Stepping in and stopping an uncomfortable interaction builds trust, and above all, I want my dog to trust that I will advocate for her.

It can be uncomfortable intervening when someone is

coming too near or actually touching your dog. Frankly, it took me a long time to find ways to stop unwanted attention. Here are a few polite phrases that I've found helpful:

- "Excuse me, we are looking for a potty area and need to move along quickly before there's an accident." And keep walking.
- "I'm so sorry! We're training right now. Excuse us." Then keep walking.
- When someone approaches, arm outstretched, and says, "All dogs love me. I'm a dog person!" I respond with, "That's wonderful, but my dog doesn't like strangers." And then keep on walking.

Sometimes advocating for our dogs is as simple as moving away, like I did with my dog at the vet office. No words, just quietly slipping away to a quiet spot to take a breath.

There is one question people ask that give me pause. "Is your dog friendly?" Of course, I want my dog to be friendly. I think she's friendly. But if a stranger were too rough petting or grabbed her head and went face to face with her, I don't know if she'd be friendly. She might be scared. If I didn't intervene quickly enough, she might act like a dog and defend herself. So, how do I answer that question? "When she's with friends and family she is very friendly. But I've taught her never to talk to strangers." I get odd looks, but it usually stops people from coming closer or laying a hand on my dog.

TEAM ACTIVITIES (AKA POTTY BREAKS)

This wouldn't be a real dog book if we didn't talk about poop. It is a universal topic among dog guardians and professionals alike. Why are we so fascinated with our dog's poop? Why are we then horrified when our dogs are so fascinated with poop? Odd. Here's a little poop trivia. At one point in my life, I lived with four Great Danes and a German Shepherd mix. Do the math: that's 600+ pounds of drooling, furry love! I could match the poop to the dog; even though they all ate the same food, everyone's poop was different. Too much information? Nah . . . responsible dog guardianship! (Or I'm just nerdy like that.)

Isn't it odd that we view our pets as "little furry people" until it comes to the universal need to poop and pee? Think about it. When we bring a puppy home, the general advice is to take the puppy outside on a leash, x number of times per day, to teach them where they may eliminate. Sound advice. Then we watch them. We might even cheer them on for pooping. Creepy!

Back inside the house, when we humans need a potty break, we head to the bathroom, which typically has conditioned air to keep the temperature just right and our feet stay warm and dry; we can close the door for privacy. But how often do we open the door to find our dog sitting and waiting for us? Or hear them whining at the door? And we find this odd behavior. But, from the dog's perspective, toileting is a team activity. We stand and watch them poop; shouldn't they return the favor? Do they find it odd that we hide to poop, but they are limited to pooping while tethered to us?

TABLE MANNERS . . . (YOUR KIBBLE SMELLS BETTER THAN MINE)

"My dog begs whenever we eat." "My dog only gets kibble, never 'human food' because I don't want my dog to beg." "Dogs should never be fed from the table." "My dog is terrible – he constantly has his paws on the counter, sniffing food."

Oh, my, so many opinions. Have you ever stopped to consider what your dog thinks when he is engaged in some of these behaviors you don't like? Is it really begging or just normal curiosity? Why do we assume that the dog is begging? Does your dog "beg" for kibble, or just food that smells delicious? I actually do not believe that the behavior people describe as "begging" is begging. So, what does it mean to beg? Oxford Languages Online puts it this way: 1) ask (someone) earnestly or humbly for something; 2) ask for something, typically food or money as a charity or a gift.

Dogs experience their world through their nose more intensely than humans do. When they smell something interesting (my lunch), they want to investigate. How do they investigate? Sniffing. So, if my sandwich is on the counter, and my dog gets a whiff of the sandwich, the most normal thing in the world is for her to walk over and investigate the delightful aroma on the counter (sniff my sandwich). Chances are, she will start drooling, too. Is that begging or investigating? Has she asked me for anything? Nope. She's investigating something interesting like any normal dog would.

Let's say that my husband also walks into the kitchen, having caught a whiff of my sandwich. He sees the sandwich and comments, "Hey, that looks good. Can I have a bite?" Who's actually begging? The human. But we don't find this offensive in the least. We might feel pretty good about ourselves because that sandwich was amazing enough that another human wanted to taste it.

But, you say, my dog drools when she sniffs the food – isn't that begging? I'd say no. Drooling is an automatic response to something that smells delicious. Begging is intentional. One meal a day, my dogs are fed kibble. They also get medication wrapped in cream cheese. They never drool over the kibble, but both dogs lie down and drool profusely when I get the cream cheese out. Even when it's got medication hidden in the center, cream cheese is clearly more pleasing to the nose than kibble. Honestly, I can barely stomach the smell of kibble. If my dogs drooled over kibble the way they drool over their home-prepared meals, I might be offended!

"When my dog is under the table during meals, he's begging!" Maybe, but there's another way to look at it. Dogs are a social species, just like humans. One of the reasons humans share our homes with dogs is because our dogs are social. So why do we banish them from the more important events in our lives? Sharing meals with friends and family is a big deal to me. Family meals are extremely rare now that my kids are grown. My husband and I have different schedules, too, so a shared meal with another human only happens two or three times a week, sometimes less. That my dogs hang around the table when I eat is welcome. In fact, they are reinforced for being near me, lying on their rugs, and keeping me company. Sometimes they get crunchy dog cookies while I eat. What's the difference between a crunchy cookie and a cookie? Crunchy cookies are just that, crunchy. I use them when I want my dog to take her time chewing. When I'm training, I use small treats that can be eaten quickly so we can train efficiently. If I give my dog a big, crunchy cookie while were working on jumping over, then training will progress more slowly because I'm waiting for her to chew the crunchy cookie. Small, soft treats (cookies) are eaten quickly so we can move on with training. Sound silly? It may, but that's what I do with my dogs.

Other times they get bits of what I'm eating. Is my dog interested in the enticing odors wafting from my food? Is my dog simply being social and wanting to be near me? It's probably a little bit of both and possibly other motivating factors that I've not thought of. The bottom line: is it beneficial to assume that normal doggy behavior is necessarily bad behavior? No. A different approach is recognizing that normal doggy behavior may simply be incompatible with what humans consider appropriate.

It's hard to see things through the eyes of another person, yet most people try. When a friend is sharing a story or a problem, we try to see it from their perspective. But, how often do we stop and think about things from our dog's perspective? If we don't, we may fall into the trap of assuming the worst about our dogs. Is the dog really begging or just being social? Probably the latter. And then there are those odd behaviors that seem universal to humans and are just weird from the dog's perspective, like back slapping and hugging. How does our dog interpret these natural tendencies? Watch your dog closely. He's telling you exactly how he feels.

6

MY DOG'S PROBLEM BEHAVIOR...(I LOVE MY DOG, EXCEPT WHEN...)

Many of the clients I work with contacted me because of problem behavior. But what is problem behavior? What may seem like a problem in one context may be desirable in another. The dog who fixates on an odor and won't give it up could be great at competitive nose-work or search and rescue, but it could be a problem behavior for the person just wanting to walk the dog down the street. Broadly speaking, the problem behaviors I work with most often with clients fall into four categories.

SCENARIO 1: DOG'S NATURAL, OR NORMAL, BEHAVIOR IS INCOMPATIBLE WITH HUMAN EXPECTATIONS

This is probably the most frustrating for both person and pet. It's the primary cause of miscommunication and tension in multi-species homes. Internalizing the fact that your dog is first and foremost a dog is critical. Dogs do doggie things. They are genetically driven to forage, urine mark, alert bark, protect themselves from perceived threats, protect resources (food, shelter), vocalize, explore, dig, jump, chase, be uncomfortable with any restriction or confinement that prevents normal behavior (leashes, small spaces), and drink from toilets.

Yep, you're living with a different species. Expect your dog to behave in a manner that is consistent with his species. This alone prevents most of the frustration people have with their dogs. I heard Dr. Patricia McConnell, author of *The Other End of The Leash* and *Educating Will*, comment that when her dog is doing something she doesn't like, she gets curious. She asks herself why he's doing what he's doing. I love that perspective. First, it validates me. I spend a lot of time wondering why my dog does what she does. Second, it focuses attention on the behavior, not the dog. It prevents judging the dog for being a dog.

"My dog is stubborn" is a common phrase I hear from dog owners. When I ask, "What does that mean to you?" the general response is something like, "My dog doesn't do what I tell him to do." It may be that the dog doesn't come when called or won't stop barking. What does stubborn mean? The *Oxford Languages Online* says stubborn is having or showing dogged determination not to change one's attitude or position on something, especially in spite of good arguments or reasons to do so. If stubborn is an attitude or opinion, does this apply to a dog who won't come when called? Maybe not.

Opinions are very difficult to change. When was the last time you were successful in changing your parent's, partner's, or friend's opinion when you commanded them to change? But changing behavior can be easier. If my dog doesn't come when called, I need to consider her motivation. What would motivate a dog to comply with an owner's request (cue/command)? Unlike changing an opinion, motivation is something we can address.

"My dog counter-surfs" is another complaint I often hear.

Opportunity knocked, and your dog opened the door. Dogs are opportunistic. They have no idea that the ham on the counter was for Thanksgiving dinner. What they saw was HAM. Right. On. The. Counter. OMG! HAM! RIGHT THERE! And then they took the entire ham. But, you say, I feed them every day. I give them bones to chew. I walk them. They get enrichment. Why would they need to take food off the counter? They should know better. (Or they know not to do that.)

In your dog's mind, she sees and acts on the opportunity. It's not theft; she doesn't understand why you're so upset about the ham. And when you get upset, she's not acting guilty. She's trying to appease you. Really, there is no connection for her between her taking the ham and you getting angry. This is a classic example of miscommunication between the species. How can we address counter-surfing? This is more about adjusting your expectation about your dog and managing the environment and less about training.

Counter-surfing is an example of several species-specific behaviors combined with motivation and reinforcement. Why would your dog put his paws on the counter? He's motivated. He may smell something interesting. Or he may see you doing something with your hands on the counter or near the sink, then jump up. Remember, dogs are social. They are often curious about what their person is doing. Even when we tell our dogs to put their feet on the floor, understand that the cue *off* (feet on floor) is specific to that moment. The next time you're at the counter, your dog is likely to jump up again.

What other reasons might a dog have for jumping on the counter? Curiosity is one reason. Another possibility is that your dog wants to be involved with what you're doing. Let's consider this from the dog's perspective.

We already know that Ursa frequently does kitchen patrol. She's checking things out, on the lookout for anything out of

4

7

3

place. When I'm working at the kitchen counter, she often walks up and watches. She may watch me wash dishes, wipe off the stove, make coffee, fill my water glass, or prepare food. This isn't counter-surfing. It's observation. It's curiosity. Years ago, when our first Great Dane, Lucy, was with us, a trainer harshly criticized me for letting my dog be in the kitchen at the counter. This was many years before I ever thought about becoming a professional dog trainer. Following the trainer's advice, I began shooing the dogs away from the counter and out of the kitchen. I never felt good about this, but I was trying very hard to do the right thing for my dog. As I've learned more about dog behavior, my thoughts have changed about what right looks like. When I look at a dog, I see a sentient being with biologically driven needs. I assume the dog will be a dog and do doggie things.

The other reason dogs may jump on counters is that they are social beings. How often do we join our dog in whatever it is they are doing? If Ursa is sniffing something on a walk or in the yard, I frequently go see what she's sniffing. Partly because I'm curious, partly because I like being with my dog. During the day, Ursa is usually involved in my activities, whether we're checking on the chickens, taking the trash out, or I'm working in my office. I imagine that when she checks out what I'm doing at the kitchen counter she's doing something that seems completely natural based on our history of doing things together. The point is, rather than assume that the dog is up to no good when they jump on the counter, pause, and consider other options. Maybe they are just being curious. Or maybe they just want to be with you.

But what if you just don't want your dog to jump on the counters in the kitchen? That's reasonable. Then you need to consider what you want your dog to do instead.

I could spend hours upon hours "training" my dog not to

jump on the counter. I could resort to punishment when that fails. But punishment doesn't teach my dog what to do, so the behavior doesn't change. It just makes my dog learn to counter-surf when I'm not around to avoid the punishment. Remember, punishment doesn't teach the dog what to do. It just reduces the frequency of the behavior.

I'd rather manage the situation or teach the dog what to do in the kitchen. Keeping enticing things off the counter is one way. Sometimes teaching the humans in the house to keep the counter clean is harder than teaching the dog not to jump on the counter. Blocking the kitchen off with a baby gate is another option. I could teach the dog what to do in the kitchen (*go to place*). Counter-surfing, while annoying, is a very normal doggie behavior.

"My dog steals laundry (underwear, sox) and runs." This is a great game for a dog! We could put a positive spin on it and say it's great cardio for people and pets, but I think most people wouldn't see the humor in that. But laughter is a great option when your dog grabs a sock. Laugh at your dog, laugh at the situation, shake your head, and sigh; your dog is being a dog, doing doggie things. Walking away. Removing your attention may be the best choice you can make in those moments.

I get many calls about reactivity. Yes, it can be a problem. It can be a safety concern. Leash reactivity, door reactivity, dog reactivity – dogs are not the only reactive species. People are reactive, too.

But what is reactivity? That's a good question. I'll define it this way: reactivity is an intense response to stimuli; reactivity is a normal response to a perceived threat or potential injury or injustice; all species exhibit reactive behavior. Reactivity is a response, not a personality trait. Some individuals exhibit stronger visible responses to stimuli and may be labeled reactive. Other individuals have similar internal responses to stimuli but don't exhibit the same visible response.

Living with and managing a dog who is reactive often creates stress and stronger responses (reactivity) on the other end of the leash. An owner's response to a trigger (the doorbell, the dog) may become as intense as the dog's response. The owner, seeing a trigger ahead, may start shortening the leash, unknowingly signaling to the dog that a reaction is about to happen (i.e., the leash is getting tight, and the dog is going to be pulled backward).

SCENARIO 2: DOG'S EDUCATION IS INCOMPLETE

Education takes time. How long did it take you to learn a foreign language, calculus, or drive a car? Six weeks? More? A 6-week-long puppy class or adult obedience class, even if you practice every day between classes, is not enough time for your dog to learn everything. First, most pet owners are not professional dog trainers. You are learning how to teach your dog while you're also teaching your dog. That's not easy. Trainers make teaching look easy because we train dogs for hours a day, many days a week. We talk about training. We read about training. We take classes and go to conferences about training. We really enjoy training. You may see training your dog as another chore on your to-do list.

If you don't enjoy training your dog, then your own motivation may be lacking. The effect is less time spent educating your dog. I get that. Teaching my dog a down-stay is not really interesting to me. What motivates me to work on mundane skills, like *place*, is knowing that once the foundation skills are learned, then we can start doing more interesting things, like agility, parkour, or nosework. My need for motivation to stick with a training plan is no different than my dog's motivation to engage in training.

Does your dog really need to know everything in 6 weeks? No. When you look at that adorable 8-week-old puppy sitting in your living room chewing on your rug, take a deep breath. Really. Just stop. Don't react. Ask yourself, "Why is he chewing on the rug?" Is he lonely? Is he hungry? Is he trying to understand what a rug is? Did your partner spill a drink or drop a piece of food on that particular spot on the rug a week ago? Your puppy would probably be able to smell that. Is there a better option nearby for him to chew than your rug? What would you like your puppy to chew on instead? Is it something the puppy even likes to chew on? Sometimes we offer a puppy a chew toy that we like, but the puppy doesn't, so he goes back to the rug.

Did your newly adopted adult dog just pee in the office? Don't react. While you're cleaning up the mess, ask yourself why your dog might have done this. Really think about it, without assumptions or judgment. Why would a newly adopted dog pee in the house? There are several reasons. She's in a new environment and is feeling uncertain. You may not understand what her signal for going outside is. She may have been asking for an hour to go outside and pee, but you didn't understand her signal. That's no one's fault. That's part of the process of getting to know each other. She may have lived her life outside, where she could pee when and where she wanted to. Many dogs who were raised outdoors have a difficult time transitioning to living inside a house. Stress can lower immune function. Changing homes is stressful. She may have developed a urinary tract infection. Perhaps your previous dog, who had health issues in the last few years of life, peed in that spot. Your new dog may still smell it and think it's the indoor toilet. Resist the urge to get frustrated or to label the new dog. She is struggling to get to know you and this new environment. Not a bad dog. A dog who is in a new place and hasn't settled into her new family.

But here you are with a dog that you think should know what to do by now. Maybe you've been to one or two group classes, or you've worked with a private trainer. Your dog's been part of the family for weeks, maybe months. And your 6-month-old dog still can't walk on a leash. Yep. He's not a socially mature dog. His brain is still developing, and his body is growing rapidly. He's trying to understand and adapt to human social expectations. He's also trying to express innate behavior. He's learning human language (cues). He's developing impulse control. He's got a lot going on!

I don't expect my dog or any dog to walk well on a leash consistently until they've reached social maturity, and then only if they've had consistent, appropriate training along the way. Have any of my 100-pound, 6-month-old puppies pulled me? Yes. I have two reasons to set up leash training practice in such a way that I minimize the possibility that my giant puppy can pull me. First, I'm a petite woman. My Great Dane puppies are usually as big or bigger than I am by the time they are 6–8 months old. If my dog pulls me hard enough, I can be injured. If I'm injured, I can't teach her how to walk on a leash. Valuable time is lost. The more important reason in my mind is that I don't want her practicing undesirable behavior. When we're training outside, usually in a fenced area in the beginning, if she pulls, I can drop the leash. I can walk away. I can ignore her. I'm not in a position where I need to attempt to hold on to her because the reality for me is I cannot effectively restrain her. I accept this as part of owning a giant breed dog. So, we do a lot of practicing in a safe area where I can prevent injury to myself while teaching her leash manners.

Most of my clients have much higher expectations for their

dogs than I have for my dogs. As I've talked with other trainers, I think this is generally true. So, I'm giving you a pass. Your dog does not need to be perfect. It's okay for your dog to be cute, funny, quirky, or eccentric. It's okay if your dog gets on the furniture. It's okay if your dog gets excited at the door. It's okay to let your dog be a dog. Really. It's never too late to teach your dog to walk on a leash, come when called, or give a high-five. The most important thing is that your dog trusts you. That's not a training issue. That's a relationship issue. Once trust is broken, you may never get it back. If your dog is excited to see you, wants to be near you, is eager to do things with you, you are successful. You brought a dog home to be a companion. Do that first. We can teach skills later. Excuse me. I'm going to share a bowl of popcorn with my dog while we watch the squirrels in the yard.

SCENARIO 3: DOG HAS AN UNDIAGNOSED MEDICAL CONDITION

If a dog doesn't feel well or is in pain, you may or may not see changes in movement or behavior. When I have a headache or a cold, my behavior changes. I don't perform as well as I do when I'm healthy. When I have a headache, I feel irritable. Actually, I'm irritable if I'm hungry, too. You may not know that I'm feeling that way because I work hard to mask it. But people who know me well can usually pick up on my feelings. Our companion pets hide their feelings, too.

Remember the study I mentioned earlier that suggests that many behavior problems are related to medical conditions? While one study isn't enough to generalize to the broader population, it does give me pause. If I consider the dogs I've lived with, then this fits with my experience. Arthritis is a common malady in dogs, particularly older dogs. I can think of two of my dogs who were more irritable and more likely to snap and be snarky as they got older. Pain medication helped, but I noticed them moving away from younger dogs, having less desire to play, and even showing less desire to be petted or cuddled.

Sometimes it's hard to accept that a beloved pet is aging. With aging comes discomfort. Your dog may feel stiff and sore, so she'll lie down and get up a little slower. It may be almost imperceptible. You may not notice until someone points it out. Or you might notice that a back leg seems stiff when she walks. Or you may not. After taking several courses on canine fitness and physiology, watching many hours of how dogs move in videos, learning about dog physiology, and observing movement in dogs, I am keenly aware of movement in dogs. I am not a veterinarian and can't tell you why your dog's gate is stiff or uneven or why your dog's knee twists when he walks, but I do see it. Usually.

When I was in a class once with Ursa, the trainer asked me if Ursa had an injury. She'd noticed Ursa's back left leg seemed stiff. No, I hadn't. As I thought about it, I did remember a rather awkward landing she made when jumping down from a fallen tree on one of our parkour excursions. A few days later, Ursa had her yearly vet exam. I asked our vet to look at her leg. When the vet gently stretched her leg back, Ursa whipped her head around. When the vet did the same thing with her other back leg, Ursa didn't look back. Yes, it was painful. No significant injury, but it was uncomfortable. We limited our outings to walking on flat surfaces for a few days, and she rested more (her choice). The morning she brought her toy to me during our normal play time, I realized that she hadn't done that in many days . . . actually, since the day she had that awkward landing. When I stepped back and observed her movement, it was clear that she was experiencing discomfort, I just didn't see her signals. I'm grateful that the trainer noticed the change in Ursa and pointed it out to me.

SCENARIO 4: DOG HAS OVERWHELMING FEELINGS OF FEAR OR ANXIETY

Fear is beneficial in appropriate contexts. Fear is an emotional response. It feels real during the experience. It is a perception of threat or danger. If I'm being stalked, fear would be an appropriate response to that dangerous situation. Fear will motivate me to seek safety. Once I'm safe, the fear should subside. It may take minutes or hours, or, if it is really intense, possibly several days, but the fear should abate.

Perception is deeply personal. What triggers a fear response in me may not for you. I enjoy the sound of thunder, watching lightning, and the smell of a rainstorm. My dog, Roadie, does not. Thunderstorms trigger a strong fear response. He trembles, sometimes violently. He won't take food of any kind, even if it's mealtime. Roadie hides, usually in the shower. If that's not an option, he hides in my closet. Once the storm passes, he returns to normal quickly. There are things that help Roadie get through the storm, like wearing a Thundershirt or listening to soothing music. If I'm not home when a thunderstorm happens, he's left to suffer without the benefit of his Thundershirt or soothing music.

Is his fear rational? Not to me. He's safe inside the house. Since we adopted him, he's never had a traumatic experience during a storm. I don't know everything that he experienced during his first 3 years of life before he joined our family. Could something have scared him during a storm? It's possible. Or maybe he just doesn't like storms. In this case, why he fears thunderstorms is less important than providing support during the storm. In this situation, we're able to manage his fear by providing support.

When fear is triggered by specific situations, or the response is moderate, we can often use management plans and provide support to help the dog during the situation. One example is a dog who is frightened of children. Limiting or preventing the dog's need to be around children works most of the time. Maybe your dog is nervous during large gatherings at your house. Your dog might prefer spending the day at doggie day care or you could hire a pet sitter to care for your pet during the party are good options.

There are dogs who have more extreme responses to triggers (like storms, strangers, other dogs, or new things). What might an extreme response look like? While it varies for every dog, generally a dog who tries to flee, trembles uncontrollably, paces and/or whines continually during the event, and is inconsolable would be considered having an extreme response. When fear is extreme or there are numerous fear triggers, then working with a veterinary behaviorist and a trainer experienced in working with fearful dogs is necessary. If this describes your dog, please reach out for help. There are things we can do to help dogs with extreme fear.

CALLING THE HELPLINE . . . (WHEN YOUR RELATIONSHIP IS IN TROUBLE)

Most people experience ups and downs in their relationships. It's no different with our dogs. Often, the struggle is rooted in miscommunication and unrealistic expectations. This is particularly true for interspecies relationships. What does that look like in real life? Let's imagine the dog's perspective in three human-canine relationships struggling to live peacefully. Three dogs reaching out to a trainer for help. Sound silly? Maybe. It's common for me to see a dog who is communicating but not being understood by their human. This kind of miscommunication makes life miserable for everyone. A huge part of my role as a professional dog trainer is mediating between person and pet. These are conversations I imagine from the dogs' perspective if the dogs could speak.

TINA'S TROUBLE

"Hello. Are you the trainer?"

"Yes. How can I help?"

"Well, I've had them for, oh, about 2 years. They are very nice, most of the time. It's just this one thing. I'm at my wit's end. Every time I'm out in the yard working, they go off. First, it's the noise, you know, the vocalizing. Clearly, they can see that I'm busy. Then, usually, it's grabbing me and not letting go. Sometimes it hurts. I know, they don't mean to hurt me. Just going into the yard isn't very enjoyable anymore. I've tried everything. I was telling someone at the park about it. She suggested something really, I don't know, harsh. I'm just not sure about it. What do you think? Is there hope? Can I make them stop?"

"How long has this been going on?"

"Since day one. It's always been this way. I just don't trust them. One minute everything is fine, then, it's like they've lost their mind or something."

"Where does this happen?"

"Usually it's in the backyard, but sometimes it happens in the house. Do you think you can help?"

"It's been going on for two years. That's a long time for the behavior to be happening. By now, it's likely that it's a habit. Habits are very difficult to change. Changing habits takes patience, consistency, and time. Chances are they don't realize what they are doing wrong or that they are inflicting pain. The next step is setting up an evaluation. I'll have a better understanding of the problem behavior after I've observed them interacting with you. Would an afternoon appointment work for you?"

FRANK'S FRUSTRATION

"Hello. You were referred to me by a friend. She said you really helped her. I have this problem and I'm not sure what to do about it."

"Thank you for contacting me. Tell me what's going on."

"He really is wonderful. There are so many great things about him. I really love him, it's just the walks. He's just terrible – pulling and jerking me around. It's so frustrating! It was so bad one day that I grumbled at him. He pulled me harder! I thought about biting him, even though that sounds a little ridiculous. It's embarrassing, too. Is there any hope?"

"I'm so sorry the walks are so difficult. Yes, there are things we can do to make it much better. I have an evening appointment available next Tuesday. Would that work for you?"

DAPHNE'S DILEMMA

"Um, hi, uh, you're a trainer, right?"

"Yes, I am. How can I help?"

"I don't know if there's hope. I'm ready to give up, maybe even rehoming. I'm really afraid. Nothing I do helps. The aggression is getting worse. I'm afraid I'm going to be really hurt. It's like walking on eggshells. The least little thing sets her off. When she's like that, I try to move away, I don't know, maybe she needs a break or something. Do you work with aggression? Can you teach her not to be aggressive?"

"I'm so glad you contacted me. Yes, I do work with aggression. Let's meet next Wednesday afternoon. Would that work for you?"

How do our dogs interpret our human behavior? Do they ever think we're aggressive? Do we confuse them or cause them to fear us? Sometimes we do. I believe that it's unintentional. Most dog owners love their dogs deeply. You do or you wouldn't be spending your valuable time reading this book. But our dogs don't necessarily understand intent. They are better equipped to understand our body language and our actions. They're view of the world is based on safe vs. unsafe paradigm. What was the resolution for these dogs and their people? Let's find out.

TINA'S TROUBLE

Tina is a happy-go-lucky beagle mix. She was adopted when she was about 6 months old. We don't know much about her life before she went into rescue. There is some indication that she was abandoned on the street, or maybe she was a stray. Like many beagles, Tina really enjoys digging. Digging helps her release energy, investigate the environment, and, frankly, it's just fun. It's great exercise, especially on days when her neighborhood walk is short, or she doesn't get a walk at all. On those days, she just sits in the house. She's learned that her people don't like her to be energetic inside, so she saves it for the yard. When she's digging, it's her time to just be a dog. It's her job!

Unfortunately for Tina, her humans don't like holes in the yard. When she digs, which is every time she goes outside, her humans yell at her. She's picked up some of the sounds – NO! STOP! GET OVER HERE! – but she has no idea what those words mean, so she keeps digging. Tina is so engrossed in digging that she doesn't always hear her human approach her. Once the human gets to her, her collar is grabbed, and she's pulled backward, then dragged into the house. It hurts her neck to be dragged by her collar. It's hard to breathe when she's being pulled by her collar. Tina has growled a few times. Then she gets jerked by the collar harder.

From Tina's perspective, she's behaving in a completely normal way. Dogs enjoy digging. They dig to find things, to smell, to make a spot to cool off in the summer – it's normal behavior. And it causes tension between person and pet if the person doesn't want the dog to act like a dog (digging).

Tina is a young adult. She has lots of energy and needs to burn it off. Generally, dogs can burn off energy by barking, digging, playing, foraging, chewing, walking, exploring, participating in sports, and training. Based on the available options, the dog will choose something. Ensuring that the options easily available are acceptable and species-appropriate is the responsibility of the human. After all, humans are in complete control of the dog's life for the life of the dog. Providing appropriate options for digging, foraging, barking, exercising, resting, chewing, playing, and exploring prevents undesirable behavior.

Tina's story had a happily-ever-after moment. Her people did hire a trainer. Their initial goal was to put a stop to the digging. Once they understood Tina's needs as a dog, they made a few changes and adjusted their expectations. First, Tina's dad built a legal digging zone. It was a large, raised bed, filled with dirt. Then special things were buried: a bone, a ball, a few treats. Whenever Tina would start to dig in the yard, her people would call her name, then walk over to the "legal" digging zone and drop a few treats inside. Tina learned quickly and now digs legally. To keep things interesting for Tina, her people pile dead leaves into the digging zone in the fall, fresh cut grass during the summer months, and periodically hide something interesting for her to find.

They also realized that Tina lacked regular exercise and enrichment. Now, most days of the week, Tina gets a minimum of a 30-minute walk in the neighborhood. At least twice a week, Tina goes on a field trip: group class for fun (tricks and nosework are particular favorites) and time exploring nature, usually on a long lead. Tina's family noticed that once they started field trips and regular walks Tina actually spent less time digging. Everyone's quality of life improved.

FRANK'S FRUSTRATION

Frank is an 18-month-old Bernedoodle. He was supposed to be a mini. He weighs 85 pounds. He's not overweight. And he's not a mini. So, when he pulls on a leash, well, you get the idea. Leash walking has always been challenging. When Frank was a puppy he would freeze on walks, refusing to move forward, sometimes lying flat on the ground. His owner tried encouraging him, coaxing him, and then finally resorted to pulling Frank along. As Frank got older, he started pulling, usually to sniff something, sometimes to move away from something that scared him. When Frank pulled, even if he needed to pee, his owner would "correct" Frank: a sharp jerk on the leash. This hurt Frank's neck, confused him, and made him afraid of his person, especially during leash walks. But it didn't teach him what to do.

Frank's owner had been very excited to get a puppy. He wanted a medium-sized dog, 45 pounds max, and a dog who didn't shed. He'd met a few "doodles" and thought they were cool dogs. He spent several months looking for a doodle puppy.

When a Bernedoodle (Bernese Mountain Dog/Poodle cross) became available, he was all in.

Like most people, Frank's owner had a job. Some days he worked from home. Some days he went to his office. On those days, Frank's owner asked his neighbor to come over to let Frank out to potty.

Watching training videos on YouTube and TikTok seemed like a great way to learn to train Frank. Frank's owner learned that Frank needed to submit to him and that he should be "corrected" when Frank did anything his owner didn't like. This confused Frank because he never learned what his owner wanted him to do. If Frank growled at his owner when he put his hand in the food bowl, Frank's food was taken away. Then he'd be hungry all day. Frank had no idea why his owner stole his food. Frank did learn that it was better to avoid his owner when possible.

The only problem, in Frank's owner's mind, was the leash walk. He'd tried a number of different things to make Frank walk on a leash correctly: a martingale collar, a choke chain, a prong collar. Nothing seemed to work. Now it seemed like the minute they walked outside, Frank would start pulling like crazy until they got home. Frank just wanted to get the walk over with because it wasn't fun – it was painful and confusing.

Frank's owner was exasperated with Frank. He was telling a friend about all the different things he'd tried. He was wondering if Frank was too dumb to learn something simple like leash walking. Frank's owner said he was thinking about getting an e-collar (shock collar). He saw it online, but he really didn't want to spend more money on another tool that probably wouldn't work. His friend told him about a trainer she'd been working with and suggested that he give her a call.

Frank's owner set up an appointment with the trainer. When the trainer arrived, Frank greeted like a normal adolescent dog – jumping, bouncing, and a little mouthing. Frank's owner immediately grabbed Frank's collar, jerked him down, and forced him to sit. The trainer said hello and asked the owner to let Frank go. The owner warned the trainer that Frank was big and might hurt her. She smiled and said she'd take a chance.

Frank did jump, but when his feet hit the ground, the trainer reinforced him with food. After several repetitions, Frank was starting to get the idea. He would start to jump, then stop, and then he got food. When he jumped, he didn't get anything. He was starting to learn that his behavior did matter. He could do something to get a cookie. Frank's owner was surprised when Frank's jumping decreased so suddenly without being told what to do or being forced into a sit position.

During the consult, the trainer identified a few simple things that Frank's owner could do immediately. First, add enrichment every day: sniffing, foraging, chewing, and exploring. Second, skip the walks for a while. Instead, the trainer suggested doing some trick training and fitness work, and asked Frank's owner to consider doing a group class like parkour or nosework. Walking wasn't beneficial for Frank or his owner at the moment. Third, use mealtime for problem-solving. Rather than putting that boring kibble in a bowl, the trainer asked Frank's owner to scatter feed, put the kibble in a cardboard egg carton, or fill a treat ball and let Frank roll it around to get his food. Finally, the trainer suggested that Frank and his owner meet her at her training facility (a neutral spot) to do leash training. Working in a neutral place helped Frank feel safe. The trainer also suggested trying a harness.

Frank's owner started providing him enrichment activities, but not consistently. Day training worked better for Frank's owner, so the trainer began working with Frank 3 days a week and with both Frank and his owner 1 day a week. Frank continued being fed out of a bowl.

After 2 weeks of training, Frank's owner started seeing a difference. The walks improved but still weren't perfect. Frank's owner told the trainer that some days Frank was really great. After talking a bit more, they discovered that Frank's great days had something in common: enrichment. Enrichment let Frank engage in normal doggie behavior (sniffing, foraging, digging), which seemed to lower Frank's arousal level. When Frank was calmer, the walks were better.

Several months went by after Frank completed his day training program. The trainer saw Frank and his owner at a local park. Frank was still an excited adolescent, but he was excited and polite. His leash-walking skills had improved, too. Frank and his owner were doing more things together, improving their quality of life and relationship.

DAPHNE'S DILEMMA

Daphne is about 9 months old. She's a 45-pound short haired, mixed-breed dog. She was adopted when she was about 6 weeks old. She was one of five puppies in a litter. Daphne's adopter grew up with dogs. She'd just purchased a house and was eager to finally add a canine companion to her home. Admittedly, it was a bit of a whim to get a puppy so soon. She'd gone to the shelter to look for an adult dog. And then she saw Daphne. How could she resist such a cute puppy?

Things were okay for a week or so. Potty training was the top priority. Daphne seemed to be doing well with that, but the nipping was pretty annoying. And it really hurt! While at Daphne's vet visit, Daphne's owner mentioned the nipping to the vet tech, who suggested holding the puppy's mouth shut when she bit and firmly telling her no. That sounded reasonable.

Back home, after a vet visit and a trip to the pet store, Daphne became bitey. Her owner held her mouth closed and said, "NO!" Daphne peed on the floor. Frustrated, her owner put Daphne in her crate and cleaned up the mess. Over the next few days, whenever Daphne got bitey, her owner would clamp her mouth shut, say "NO!", then Daphne peed. This was Daphne's first experience of being afraid of her owner. Her peeing was not a potty training issue. Daphne was afraid.

Over the next few weeks, Daphne's owner started seeing other behavior problems. Daphne barked at people walking past the house or when the doorbell rang, she chewed on rugs and the baseboards, and she growled when her owner put her hand in the food bowl. Her owner got advice from different people and tried everything: shaking a penny can when Daphne barked, spraying water on her when she chewed on the rugs or walls and grabbing her collar and rolling her on her back when Daphne growled. Daphne's owner enrolled her in an obedience class, but they were kicked out because Daphne barked through the entire class. Her owner's dream of a canine companion was unraveling; Daphne's dream of a happy home was, too.

During a vet visit, Daphne's owner mentioned all the behavior problems. She wondered if her dog needed meds. The vet suggested a trainer first and gave her the card of a local trainer. She called the trainer and set up a behavior evaluation.

During the behavior evaluation, the trainer noticed that Daphne had very few toys and no "legal" objects for chewing. She also noticed that Daphne displayed behavior that indicated some internal conflict – she wanted to approach the new person but then shrank back and tried to make herself small in hopes of being unnoticed.

The trainer explained that the many things Daphne's owner tried had confused Daphne. Some of the tactics were actually scary to the dog, making the human appear unpredictable and violent. Her owner was shocked. She never wanted to frighten her dog! She just wanted a nice puppy.

After talking about the goals Daphne's owner had for Daphne, like leash walking manners, greeting people nicely, going to the farmer's market, and maybe patio dining, the trainer talked about goals Daphne might have, such as digging, chewing, exploring, barking, playing, and feeling safe. Next, the trainer talked about how to achieve their goals while building Daphne's confidence and feelings of security.

First, the trainer suggested giving Daphne choices. Choice-making is critical for resilience. Dogs who are resilient are able to adjust to a variety of situations. Daphne's owner wanted to take Daphne with her when she went out into the community. For success, Daphne needed to be flexible in different places. That flexibility starts with choice-making at home. Training games were introduced as well as exploratory walks. To her surprise, Daphne's owner loved going on exploratory walks with her dog. She found it as relaxing for her as it seemed to be for Daphne.

Next, the trainer suggested options for Daphne's (new) toy boxes. Toy boxes provide opportunities for dogs to dig, explore, and, yes, make choices. A variety of toys was included in each of Daphne's toy boxes: rubber type, squeaky type, antlers, bull horns, soft plush toys, ropes, tugs, and balls. Initially, Daphne's owner didn't want to include plush toys because Daphne would shred them. The trainer assured her that this was both normal and desirable. Shredding a toy was a great way to prevent shredding the rugs. It provided an approximation of normal dog behavior.

At first, Daphne didn't interact with her toy boxes. The

trainer suggested tossing a few treats into the toy box for Daphne to "find." That did the trick! Soon Daphne was spending time digging in her toy box. To her delight, Daphne's owner reported that Daphne was bringing toys to her to solicit play. Soon they had regular play sessions initiated by Daphne. Daphne had stopped chewing on the rugs. Daphne's submissive peeing stopped. She even snuggled with her owner now. Both person and pet were more relaxed and were enjoying their time together.

As Daphne's confidence grew, her owner noticed that teaching new things, like leash walking and tricks, became more enjoyable. Daphne was eager to learn, in fact, she learned things really fast! Having learned the basic stuff during the private training sessions, Daphne's owner asked the trainer what else she could do with Daphne. The trainer suggested starting with a nosework or parkour class.

Daphne's owner sent an update to the trainer. Over the next year, Daphne and her owner spent time together – hiking, going for exploratory walks (still a favorite for both), and trying out different group training classes.

These stories represent an amalgam of clients and dogs I've seen over the years. The most common problem isn't the dog. It's the normal struggle of living in a multi-species home. Dogs are dogs. They will act like the species that they are. Dogs do things that make humans uncomfortable, like sniffing poop or exploring dead carcasses. Dogs do things that frighten humans, like growling, barking, and mouthing. Dogs do things that annoy people, like jumping, digging, and counter-surfing. We can't train a dog to ignore their biology. We can scare them into shutting down and stop openly displaying normal behavior. But that is not training. Suppressing behavior may look like a good idea, but it causes suffering for your dog. And scaring that dog into suppressing normal behavior creates fear and distrust of people. I've not met anyone who wants their dog to be afraid of them. Rather than suppressing normal doggy behavior, ethical trainers will offer solutions for letting dogs express normal doggy behavior in a way that is compatible with living in a human home.

7
CANINE EDUCATION...
(TRAINING ISN'T ENOUGH)

All dogs need obedience training, right? Nope. In my opinion, what most people consider obedience training (*sit, down, stay, heel*) for companion pets probably won't set you or your dog up for success. Obedience training doesn't include enough skills for day-to-day life with your dog. There are many more skills your dog needs to be successful as a companion pet than are covered in obedience training.

IF NOT OBEDIENCE, THEN WHAT?

What is obedience training, anyway? Typically, when people say their dog needs obedience, they want their dog to be compliant. This is frustrating to me as a trainer. When I think of obedience my first thought is that obedience is a competitive sport. It takes years to train dogs for success in obedience trials. Most people don't know that. Many people think one or two obedience classes will produce a compliant dog. That's unrealistic and frustrating.

Traditional obedience training includes skills like sit, down, stay, retrieve, and heel, all with distractions, distance, and duration. Distractions are the wild card of any training, whether its general manners or competitive sports training. Distance and duration are about the dog's ability to perform. Distractions are external, outside of the control of the dog. The distraction is why your dog can do a perfect recall inside your home and it falls apart the minute you step outside. Distraction is what makes performing so difficult.

Don't all dogs need these skills? Possibly. I'm not saying that you shouldn't teach them to your dog. What I am saying is that they aren't enough. People who take their dogs to one or two group classes and think that's enough often disappointed. They may think that their dog is "stubborn" or "stupid" when in reality, the dog probably didn't learn the skills needed to be successful in the family.

The reality is no human child could learn all the skills and information needed in 12 weeks to be a successful adult. Dogs are not that different. It takes time and practice to learn new things. Plus, dogs have a distinct disadvantage when living with a human: they don't know the language or the cultural norms of living with humans. They are expected to learn how to understand humans, learn cultural norms (don't pee in the house, don't jump on people, don't counter-surf, don't, don't, don't), ignore their species-specific inclinations, and accept all human interaction before they're a year old. Sound impossible? It is.

THE WELL-EDUCATED DOG

Rather than focusing solely on "obedience," I'd love to see the conversation shift to the idea of educating our dogs. Why? I think it describes what we need to be doing. Education helps us look at the dog as a learner. And they are. Dogs learn all the time, whether we realize it or not. Another reason I prefer to think of training as educating the dog is that it gives us an opening to talk about skills that your dog needs to be successful in your home. Some traditional obedience skills taught in group classes are never used at home or are used so infrequently that when the skill is needed, the dog doesn't remember how to do it. The human may not remember the exact cue taught in the group class – it happens! *Down-stay* is one example. That's actually two different behaviors, but they're often combined. How often does your dog need to *down-stay* at home? Daily? Weekly? Only when guests come to the door? (Hint: your dog will not be able to do this easily even if he has a great *down-stay* in class.)

But there is something you do need more often. How often do you need your dog to *settle* on their bed or mat? Every day? During Zoom calls or dinner? Probably. A *settle* on a mat is different than the traditional *down-stay*. *Settle* is a relaxed posture (soft, curved body, soft facial features, slow wagging or still tail) that includes a calm emotional state. A traditional *down-stay* is an alert posture: head erect, ears up, and tension in the body. The dog is ready for the next cue rather than hanging out in the family room.

How long should it take to train your dog? That depends. You could probably teach your dog to *sit* in the house in about 5 seconds; *sit* to get her food bowl in a couple of days or maybe a week; *sit* and let strangers pet or touch – in months, a couple of years, sometimes never.

Training will not teach a dog to enjoy being social. How social your dog is depends on genetics (the breed or breed mix), learning (history of social interaction beginning at birth), environment (which includes the time of day, specific location, and who the interaction is with), and self (who they are as individuals). Sociability is a spectrum. Not every dog will tolerate strangers touching them, while others thrive on human touch.

I relate to the former. I don't like people I've just met touching me. I tolerate handshakes because I'm expected to in certain circumstances, not because I like them. I've taught myself to take a deep breath, plaster a smile on my face, and get through social greetings. That person who leans into me while shaking my hand I avoid at all costs in future encounters. Too close for comfort! Fear of getting sick is not the underlying reason I shrink back from social events. I have a very large personal space bubble. Looking at me, knowing that I work one-on-one with people professionally, most people have no idea how I'm feeling internally. That has taken years of practice. Dogs have personal space bubbles, too. While I can run to the ladies' room if I need a break from people, dogs are tethered to their person and cannot escape. Getting to know and then advocate and respect your dog's personal space bubble will go a long way toward your dog learning to trust you.

For many people, it's a high priority for their canine companion to walk on a leash politely. Leash walking is far more complex than most people realize. Achieving a walk that is enjoyable for both person and pet can take months or a couple of years. Your dog may have great leash walking skills but not enjoy the walk. Your dog may have average or below-average leash skills, and you may both enjoy the walk. Walking skills vary according to the context. On a trail walk, my dog may be able to walk ahead or behind me on a 6-, 10-, or 30-foot leash. When walking in a downtown area, she's on a shorter leash and must walk next to me. Sometimes. But not always. The number of obstacles (people, trash cans, etc.) on the sidewalk may allow more freedom of movement and a longer leash. It's up to me to determine where she needs to be in proximity to me based on the environment.

Door greetings are another source of owner frustration. What do you want your dog to do? Sit? Why? What is the simplest thing your dog could do successfully? How about standing next to you? She's much more likely to succeed at this than sitting in a highly arousing situation. Why does teaching a polite door greeting seem so difficult? Because most of us don't have enough people coming to the front door to practice effectively. That's the primary reason. If you don't practice enough, the skill won't be learned (fluency). If I said that you needed to practice polite door greeting (staying a few feet away from the door, standing still, and waiting) about a thousand times, how long would it take for your dog to practice that many times? Once the skills were taught (where to stand/sit/lie down, how long to hold that position, what to do when released from that position), if you had one person come to your house once a week, it would take 19 years to practice a thousand times. Even if you needed to practice a hundred times, that would still take 2 years if you only practiced once a week.

Yes, your dog can learn what to do and where to go, but the real key to a great door greeting is repetition until fluency is achieved. Fluency is the ability to perform the skill or task under conditions that include distance, duration, and distractions. Door greetings are highly arousing and often startling for your dog. Then add your own arousal to the situation, and you have the perfect recipe for chaos. How committed are you to practicing enough to achieve fluency? Sometimes managing the situation is more realistic. And that's okay. Really. Giving you and your dog a pass on being perfect at the door may be the better option.

Educating (training) your dog takes time. It cannot be

rushed. While teaching your dog life skills, you're also teaching your dog about the relationship she'll have with you and other people. Can she trust you to prevent strangers from mugging her, or is it up to her to defend herself from strangers touching her? Do you like spending time with her, or are you angry or frustrated when you're together? Can she trust you to explain (teach) her what to do in new situations?

What's the best way to educate my dog?

I wish every dog owner would ask that question! The very first thing to decide is what you want to do *with* your dog. How do you imagine life with your dog? Write it down. Then, start contacting trainers.

Dog training and behavior consulting is an unregulated industry. That means anyone can call themselves a dog trainer, regardless of their level of education or experience. Look for a trainer who is certified. That indicates a basic level of professional knowledge. A trainer who loves dogs but has only trained their own dog may or may not have the necessary knowledge, experience, or resources to help you with your dog.

Certified trainers are required to take continuing education courses (CEUs) to maintain their certification. Ask potential trainers what CEUs they're working on or have recently completed. We will be thrilled you asked and happy to tell you all about it. By the way, if you talk with a trainer who doesn't think they need ongoing education or is hesitant to talk about new things they are learning, then consider that a red flag. New discoveries about animal behavior and how to improve welfare are being made. We know so much more than we did even 10 years ago. Humane trainers spend time keeping up with best practices for animal training and welfare.

Professional dog trainers have preferences. Each of us has particular kinds of dogs or skills that we really love teaching. While professional trainers are skilled in teaching all breeds and all ages, as well as working with people, most of us have some sort of specialty. If you have a giant breed dog or a dog who doesn't give you the time of day, call me – I LOVE working with those dogs. Looking for a trainer who enjoys teaching tricks? I can do that, but I'll probably suggest working with one of my colleagues who loves trick training. Do you have a puppy? We all love working with puppies! The point is, asking potential trainers what they enjoy will help you determine if that trainer is a good fit for you and your dog.

In addition to identifying a trainer you would like to work with, you will need to decide on how training is delivered: group classes, private training, day training, board and train, or some combination. There are pros and cons to each option.

Group classes that teach general manners are by far the most economical way for you to train basic skills. The added benefit of a group class is meeting other people and dogs. Seeing other people going through the same process that you are can be encouraging. Most basic group classes will cover things like *recall, sit, down, stay/wait, targeting, stationing, drop it/leave it,* and some leash walking. You'll meet weekly and be given homework. In smaller classes (six or fewer handler and dog teams), the trainer may be able to provide additional help for your specific needs, but that's not always the case.

There are downsides to group classes. First, the curriculum is generic. The same skills are taught to all dogs, regardless of the needs of the family or dog. Every handling team learns skills at the same time. This may or may not meet your specific needs.

What most dog owners want is skill plus fluency. Fluency results when a skill has been proofed. This means the skill can be performed in a variety of contexts that include distractions, the dog can maintain a behavior for some amount of time or duration, and the dog can comply with the cue at some distance (if applicable). Fluency requires multiple sessions of group classes. Group classes are generally 6 weeks. If your goal is fluency, then let's say that your dog needs three classes (that would be a bare minimum; most dogs need more). That's 18 weeks of going to class consistently. Assuming you can register for three classes in a row. You may have work obligations, personal travel plans, or your dog may need to recover from surgery during that time. Or you may find that intermediate or advanced classes are only offered quarterly. That initial 5-month time frame could stretch to a year. That's neither good nor bad, but it is something to consider when choosing how to train your dog.

Private training is more flexible. You and your trainer will set training goals during intake, either at the first session or on the phone before the first session. This is often done informally, with your trainer asking questions about your lifestyle, what you would like to do with your dog, and any specific considerations that need to be accounted for, such as living with young children, a very social lifestyle, or having elderly guests.

While going through the training process, private trainers will also help you with a management plan. Living with a dog, who is a different species, does require making some concessions for the dog's well-being. In some situations, management is simply more efficient than training. A good example of this is the trash can. Yes, you can train a dog to leave the trash alone. But are you willing to spend the amount of time needed? Or would you rather move the trashcan or get a dog-proof trash can? If you choose the latter, that frees your time to work on more important skills, like polite greetings. When I taught puppy classes, the skill *drop it* was covered in week four or five. If I'm working with a client whose dog is particularly focused on putting unsafe things in their mouth, we will work on *drop it* in the first session. If I'm working with a client who doesn't have an issue with this, I may not cover it at all during private training. When working with a family with children, part of each session is devoted to teaching the children how to safely interact and play with their dog. Private training, in my experience, is the most efficient way to meet the training needs of everyone in the home.

Private training costs more upfront than group classes. You are paying for the trainer's travel time, time spent at your home teaching multiple species (you and your dog), and the time it takes her to develop a plan specifically for your family. In some cases, I'll work with multiple dogs and two or more humans. You may find that 6 or 8 weeks of private training costs more initially, but it does save time and money over group classes in the long run.

Day training is a great option that many people don't know about. The trainer works one-on-one with your dog, usually at your home or at the trainer's facility, for an hour several days a week, teaching skills that help meet your goals. It is costlier than private training. You and your dog are getting the benefit of experienced, professional training in a highly focused session. Goals are determined during the intake process. When I offer day training, I'll work with the dog 4 days a week for 1 hour. On the fifth day, I work with everyone in the family to transfer skills. Transferring skills teaches the family members how to incorporate the cues into day-to-day life with their dog. If I use the word "off" as a cue that means four feet on the ground, but someone in the family uses the word "down," the dog will be confused, and the family member might think the dog isn't learning the right thing. The benefit is that your dog is getting time with a professional trainer who has spent time honing her training skills, which can speed up the training process.

Board and train is another option for training and is the most expensive of any option and requires the least time commitment (upfront) for the owner. Your dog goes to a boarding facility for several weeks (2, 4, or 6 is common). During that time, your dog is taught skills based on your goals or the general skills taught in the board and train program. Board and train options are beneficial when an owner is recovering from an illness or injury or has a physical limitation that prevents the owner from participating in the training process.

Like every other option, board and train has a downside. As the owner, you have no control over how your dog is being cared for or trained. You are not able to monitor the day-to-day welfare of your dog. For instance, most (but not all) of the board and train programs in my area use training methods that are not recommended by The American Veterinary Society of Animal Behaviorists (AVSAB) or any professional trainer organization that adheres to humane training principles. If you're looking for a board and train program, look for one that uses humane training techniques. Inquire about their welfare and standard of care policies. Discover how they handle dogs who are struggling to learn, who won't eat, who become ill, or who are fearful in a kennel environment, or who need emergency medical care. What is the daily schedule for dogs: how much time is spent training, resting, and socializing with other dogs and people, and what is done for daily enrichment? Can you watch your dog over a webcam? If you can, that's a green flag!

Whether you choose group classes, private, day, or boarding for training, the training techniques used make a difference. In the simplest terms, training techniques can be classified as 1) teaching the dog what to do (positive reinforcement); or 2) stopping behavior (punishment). I've oversimplified the entire training framework, but that gets to the heart of it. Now, let's look at the difference. Full disclosure: I've done both types of training, and I have chosen option 1 – I teach rather than punish.

Teaching dogs what to do is, in my mind, what educating (training) dogs should be. When I'm getting to know a dog, whether it's my dog or a client's dog, my assumption is that there are skills the dog needs to learn to be successful living in a human home. While there are skills that seem universal for all companion dogs to know, like coming when called, there may also be skills that my dog needs to know that isn't necessary or important for your dog to know. It's my role as my dog's guardian to prepare her as best I can with the skills needed to be successful living in my home. In general, a dog needs to know what to do when walking on a leash, when greeting people, and when hanging out watching a movie. All of those situations require the dog to meet human expectations for social interactions. Often human expectations clash with normal dog behavior. Remember, a dog is a dog and will behave like a dog. The purpose of training is to help dogs learn how to live in a human-centered culture.

The style of training recommended by the AVSAB, and many professional trainer organizations is humane training. That includes positive reinforcement, fear-free, and force-free methods. This is the philosophy I follow. My goal is to identify what "looks right" and then teach the skills needed to succeed. What looks right for your dog may look different than for my dog.

I really enjoy the first meeting with new clients. This is the time when I get to know human and canine. That's when we talk about what is needed to set everyone up for success. Yes, we talk about what looks right for the people, but also for the dog. My goal in this meeting is determining what skills the dog needs as well as how the humans can better meet the dog's needs. The winning combination for success is often teaching skills and providing enrichment. And having fun together. Sometimes we're so focused on making the dog "obedient" that we forget why we have a dog. We forget to have fun. So, during our sessions, I often talk about playing together. If you're stressed out about your dog having less than stellar leash manners or not having a perfect recall, here's another pass. Focus on play, on having fun together. I highly recommend checking out Dr. Amy Cook's Play Way program. She does amazing things with play between humans and canines. She dramatically changed the way I play with my dogs.

During the education and training process, I also implement management to prevent the dog from learning or practicing undesirable behavior. The process should be relatively stress-free for both person and dog. That's not to say it's frustration-free. When my puppy is learning to come when called, and all of a sudden, she gets distracted by a butterfly, that's not fun, but it's usually endearing or humorous. And look for the silver lining: a puppy chasing a butterfly is cute, even when it interrupts training. Your dog is learning how to live with you, and you are learning how to live with your dog. This is the time to build a strong relationship and develop clear, cross-species communication.

The other common method is punishment. The assumption here is that your dog knows what to do but is being willful. The perceived wrong behavior needs to be corrected. Punishment does stop the behavior if it's administered precisely, using the exact amount of force needed (never too much or too little), and if it is absolutely consistent. And it has to be perceived as a punisher by the dog. A punisher is something the dog finds aversive, like pain from a shock collar or physical force, or fear of a noise like a shaken can full of pennies or the sound from an e-collar. If the action is not perceived as a punisher, then it's both ineffective and inhumane. If you're still jerking the leash after 2 years of "training," is it effective?

But back to that "wrong" behavior that needs to be addressed. If the dog is behaving like the biological being he is, which can include resisting being confined (leashes, kennels), barking at strangers, digging, and jumping, why is that wrong? Why does that earn being choked by a collar, shoved into position, or kneed in the chest? It really doesn't make any sense to punish species-specific behavior. If you don't want a dog to act like a dog, do you really want a dog? Living with another species (or another human, for that matter) is challenging. Maybe you did get a dog and found that she's just not the right kind of companion for you. That's okay. If you're in that situation, here's your pass. Returning your dog to the rescue or breeder is okay. There is no joy in life for either of you if it's just not a good fit.

Punishment used as a primary tool for training is more likely to create unintended and undesirable behavior than positive reinforcement training is. This is particularly true when you're asking a dog to ignore biological urges. Punishment may remove or stop a behavior, but that leaves a problem for your dog. What should he do instead? Let's say that you move to a new place. The language is different, and the culture is different. In your new home, it's considered rude to smile at people, but you weren't told. Every time you smile at someone, something unpleasant happens. You don't know why, it just does. Maybe you get pinched, or slapped, or screamed at. You don't know why, but soon you make the connection that smiling is linked to weird and uncomfortable things happening. So, you stop smiling. That doesn't change the fact that you want to make friends and be friendly; you just don't know how to do that in this new community. Your normal behavior stopped (smiling), but you're left without knowing what to do.

This is the tough situation companion pets find themselves in when they are punished for species-specific behaviors but not taught what to do instead.

Sometimes the intended punisher simply doesn't work. Using a spray bottle to stop barking is an example. Barney, the lab, barks at everything: dogs, people, delivery people, squirrels, sounds on the TV. When you ask for help from your Facebook community, several people suggest spraying him with a squirt bottle whenever he barks. That sounds like a good idea, so you try it. After two weeks, it feels like he's actually barking more. So, you spray him with more water, thinking you just weren't spraying him enough. Then you notice that he starts looking at you when he's barking. His tail is wagging. His mouth is wide open like he's smiling. Oops! Barney LIKES the spray bottle. He thinks it's a great game. So, he barks more because the spray bottle is really awesome. Barney also likes drinking from the water hose, playing in the sprinkler, and swimming in the lake. Water is not an effective punisher, and in fact, it's a great reinforcer. Using water in this situation actually increased the barking because Barney loves water. Yes, this exact scenario does happen.

Gidget, the Mini-Goldendoodle, on the other hand, has a different opinion of water. When she gets sprayed for barking when looking out the window, she has a very different response. The first time she was sprayed with water, the barking stopped immediately. Her owner thought she finally found the solution to the nuisance barking. She was thrilled, at first. The next time Gidget barked, she was sprayed. Gidget stopped barking and then left the room. Even better, thought her owner. And then Gidget barked at the window again. She was sprayed again. Gidget ran out of the room. This continued for several weeks – Gidget would bark, she would get sprayed, then she would run out of the room.

One day, Gidget saw the water bottle on the kitchen counter. She ran out of the kitchen. Odd, thought her owner, she's never run out of the kitchen like that. Normally, she likes lying on her bed while I'm in here. The next day, Gidget saw her owner holding the water bottle while she was walking from the kitchen to the living room. Gidget ran in the other direction. When her owner called her, Gidget would not come. Now that is odd, thought her owner. She always comes when I call her. Over the next few days, Gidget's owner started seeing a pattern. When Gidget saw the water bottle, she ran away. No amount of coaxing would get Gidget to come near her owner when her owner held the water bottle. Some people would laugh and think that was funny. Now, when Gidget barked out the window, all her owner had to do was show her the water bottle, and she ran away. Problem solved? No. Gidget still barked out the window, but now she was also afraid of the water bottle. Gidget's owner now had two problems: nuisance barking and fear. Gidget didn't learn what to do instead of barking, and she became fearful of something in her home.

Living in fear creates stress. When stress is ongoing, it turns into toxic stress. Toxic stress decreases the quality of life and can decrease overall health and life expectancy. Does this happen in real life? Yes. People think that if a dog is afraid of something and won't approach it, it's a good thing. The dog has learned to stay away. This is true. But living in a situation where fear is a constant is unhealthy. Fear creates uncertainty. When a dog associates fear with people, it negatively affects the person-pet relationship. I would argue that inducing fear to prevent unwanted behavior is counterproductive to educating your dog.

TRAINING . . . (EDUCATING YOUR DOG TO LIVE LIFE)

Training plans should include both enrichment and whatever skills your dog needs to succeed in your home. When creating a training plan for a client, I start with understanding what the goals are for the client. I need to understand what their expectations are for the dog. Most of the time, the expectations are reasonable, but sometimes, there is a disconnect between what the owner wants and what the dog is able to do. That can cause lots of emotions: disappointment, frustration, and sometimes denial. Continuing to believe that your dog can do something that, in truth, he cannot do leads to more frustration for both person and pet. I do understand! I was lucky enough to have several dogs in the past who helped me to socialize and prepare other dogs for adoption. When it was time for them to retire, I usually had another dog who could step into that role. I had the same plans for the last puppy I brought home; I really wanted her to work with me. But she doesn't have the temperament for that role. Was I disappointed when I finally admitted that? Of course. But we do other things together that we both enjoy. It looks like I'll just need to search for another dog who might grow up to be my partner. But what if that dog doesn't like working with me? It's a possibility. The reality is I may never find another dog to fill in for my past partners: Lucy, Melody, Muse, and Roadie. Every dog is an individual with unique capabilities and preferences. Forcing any dog into a role that is too difficult and demanding or too dull and unchallenging for the individual interferes with that dog's welfare and well-being.

Let's rethink the need for obedience training. Instead, let's focus on educating our dogs. Asking, "What are the skills my dog needs to be successful?" allows us to focus on what the need is. While there are skills that are common, like recall, there are other skills that might be more appropriate for the obedience ring, like a heel. If we focus on educating, and teaching our dogs what to do, we quickly realize that punishment doesn't meet the need. Punishment leaves our dogs with a huge problem. They're left wondering what to do. And punishing innate behavior makes no sense. When we shift the approach from training for compliance to educating our dogs in life skills, success is more likely for everyone.

PART TWO
LIVING TOGETHER –
THE MULTI-SPECIES
HOME

8

LIVING TOGETHER: THE
MULTI-SPECIES LIFESTYLE

When I meet a client for the first time, I ask, "What do you want to do with your dog?" One of the most frequently stated objectives is, "I want my dog to go everywhere with me." What if I asked the dog, "What do you want to do with your human?" The answer might be something like, "I want to hang out with them, watch the world around us, and maybe play a little tug or explore around the house together." Different species, different needs, different answers. How can we accommodate both species?

People and dogs need to eat. Mealtime can be something we share with our pets, or it can be a source of frustration. There are simple things we can do to make mealtime less stressful for person and pet. What looks right to you? Is it something your pet can succeed in doing?

In warmer months, you enjoy patio dining. Your favorite restaurant allows dogs on the patio. You've seen other people take their dogs. It looks like a lot of fun. So why not take your dog out to dinner? You get a good meal, maybe a beer, and your dog is getting socialized . . . it's a win for everyone! Or is it?

You get to the patio, and you know what to expect. You know what to do. You know how to behave: sit down in a chair, engage in conversation, order your meal, wait for your meal, and engage in more conversation. You're being social. And you're having fun.

Your dog gets to the patio. Does she know what to expect? Does she know what to do? Has she been taught what to do? From your dog's perspective, lying on the pavement while surrounded by an array of stimuli that she's not allowed to explore is not fun. It's frustrating. All that stimulation is not relaxing, in fact, it can be extremely difficult to remain calm and "well-mannered."

Recently I went to dinner with my daughter. When we arrived at the pub, I noticed that three people had brought their dogs to dinner. As we ate, I observed the dogs and their people. It's fascinating to me how people and their dogs share experiences together.

Doggie Number 1, a large mixed breed, stayed near his people and was somewhat relaxed. From time to time, he would shift his position, but he remained in his place. At one point, I saw him scoot out of the way of a person walking behind him. He seemed to be an experienced patio diner, aware of his environment and his body, and able to make subtle adjustments as needed. Both of his owners frequently interacted with him, petting, and giving treats and making sure his water bowl was full. They all seemed to be enjoying themselves.

Doggie Number 2, a medium-sized doodle, enjoyed the attention she got from people. At first, it seemed like things were going well. Her owner talked with passers-by and encouraged his dog to "Go say hi" to people. He occasionally talked to his dog, telling her to *sit* or *down* or *don't bark*. Her leash was loose, and she had some freedom to walk around.

But when she saw some other dogs, she barked and lunged. Her owner scolded her, pulled her back with her leash, and finally picked her up to prevent her from getting close to other dogs. Being lifted off the ground prevented her from lunging, but it didn't stop the barking. Once the dogs moved past, she was set back on the ground. For the rest of the time, I was there (two hours), she panted, paced, and stayed alert. Her owner occasionally told her to lie down and be still. She wasn't having fun by the end of dinner. I'm not sure her owner noticed her growing distress.

Doggie Number 3, a blond Labrador retriever, sat at a table with his owner. They were seated near a busy walkway near Doggie Number 2. The blond lab was struggling on the patio. He seemed friendly, wanting to move toward people and dogs as they passed by him. But he was not allowed to greet people. He was told to *leave it* if he looked up at the approaching wait-staff. I'm not sure what the dog was supposed to *leave*. As time passed, the blond lab grew more restless. He couldn't lie down because the leash was kept very short. He was unable to shift positions or move out of the way of people walking near him. A waitperson brought a bowl of water, but the lab was unable to reach it because the leash was too short. As time went on, each time the lab tried to move, his owner would shove his butt toward the ground, ever more forcefully, while pulling his leash tighter. The dog couldn't sit without being choked by the collar. I don't think the owner was aware that his dog couldn't physically sit because the leash was so short. No one at that table was enjoying dinner.

From my perspective, Doggie Number 1 was well-educated, and his human companions were aware of his needs. They divided their attention between human conversation and brief interactions with their dog. While I don't know the dog's age or background, I'd guess he was socially mature, probably three years or older. He was calm but alert, confident, and easy-going. He was the poster dog for what most people want when they say, "I want my dog to go everywhere." Shouldn't every dog be like Doggie Number 1? No. Every dog is an individual. Doggie Number 1 had the precise temperament paired with the skills needed for that situation. He also had human companions who checked in with their dog frequently enough to ensure he was doing okay. In short, they were sharing the patio dining experience.

As a stranger observing Doggie Number 1, I don't have the full story. Perhaps Doggie Number 1 had extreme separation anxiety and couldn't be left alone. It's possible that he was calm and relaxed only if he was with his people. We don't know. I have had clients whose dogs had separation anxiety. During treatment, the dog wasn't left alone. That's the standard protocol for many separation anxiety cases. It's also extremely hard to do. One client I remember very well spent as much time teaching her dog what to do at her office, when dining out, and going to the hardware store as she did working on the separation anxiety exercises I assigned because leaving the dog at home wasn't an option most of the time. For this dog, safety and security were tied to being with her owner.

What about Doggie Number 2? Things seemed to be going so well. One of the challenges is that dogs may have the skills to go places with their owner, but their level of tolerance to stimuli is more limited than their owner is aware of. Doggie Number 2 clearly enjoyed engaging with people but not dogs. Is that a training issue? Possibly. It could be that Doggie Number 2 likes dogs when she's off-leash in an area where she can make choices. It could be that the leash prevented her from interacting in a normal doggie way. Another possibility is that she generally likes patio dining, but on that particular night, she was tired, had an ear infection, had been to the groomer earlier in the day, or had just come from daycare. In other words, maybe she just wasn't feeling social and had no choice. She was stuck in a place she didn't want to be. Have you ever felt that way? I have, and it's miserable.

Our ability to tolerate environmental stimulation fluctuates. The same is true for our dogs. On days that I feel good physically and mentally, I'm more likely to want to go out. But I have limits. There are certain restaurants that I don't go to anymore, even though the food might be good. I'm sensitive to environmental stimulation. Noise is a particular challenge for me. There were days when I worked in a shelter when the noise drove me mad. During the day, I'd take breaks from the noise by taking a dog for a walk outside or taking a dog on a car ride. I loved my job, but the noise was intolerable. I can only imagine how the noise affected the dogs in the shelter, who were sound-sensitive but couldn't escape the noise.

Managing noise levels is a normal part of my life. When I designed my training facility, I included acoustic panels to reduce noise. Rubber flooring was installed because it absorbs sound better than epoxy or tile flooring. A box fan is available to help mask the noise from outside during training classes. I have fountains and aquariums in my home in almost every room, along with numerous houseplants, which also help absorb sound. Yes, it looks nice. But there's a practical reason for this. Traffic noise, particularly the sound of some motorcycles, is intolerable. It makes me tense and anxious. There are times when I feel the need to flee to safety when the traffic sounds are too intense or constant. I can tolerate much more stimulation first thing in the morning, but by evening, I've usually had enough and want the safety of my quiet home. I'm able to make adjustments to my home and workspace because I have the ability to make choices to some degree. Our canine companions often don't have the freedom to manipulate their environment to meet their needs.

Our modern world can be tough for dogs to live in. Dogs can be overwhelmed by sensory input, just like people. I think we don't recognize this in dogs nearly enough. In considering the patio dining experience, a dog may be overwhelmed by the barrage of noise. As I think about one of my favorite patio dining spots, background noise would include vehicles going by (cars, trucks, motorcycles, trains), music (live bands or recorded), dishes clanking, human voices, dogs barking, and in the fall, the sound of the propane heaters going. Those are sounds my human ears can identify. But what about a dog? Dogs can hear a wider range of frequencies than humans. They are able to detect higher frequencies, making the sound of things like vacuum cleaners and power tools more intense for dogs than for people. This contributes to the common problem of dogs barking at the vacuum. The sound of the vacuum might be irritating or physically uncomfortable. I wonder how the constant noise our dogs live with affects our dogs' ability to just be calm. If a dog is patio dining and starts getting restless, could sound be a contributing factor? Yes. Doggie Number 2 may have been experiencing the effect of being overstimulated and just needed to retreat to a quiet place.

Doggie Number 3 struggled the most. He appeared to be younger, possibly adolescent, somewhere between 9 months and 2 years. I'm just guessing, really. He had that gangly look of adolescence. Assuming he was an adolescent, one question is, did his owner think this was the way to socialize his dog? Possibly. It's also possible that this was not the normal routine for the dog and owner, but for some reason, they needed somewhere to go that was dog friendly. Perhaps there were repairs going on at their home, and they needed a place to hang out for a few hours. We just don't know. We do know that the dog had no idea what to do in that environment, and his owner didn't know what to do with the dog. It's also clear that the dog's needs were not being met, which only added to his discomfort. Holding the leash tight enough to prevent the dog from being physically comfortable added to the dog's restlessness. Withholding water, except for medical reasons, is never acceptable.

So, was this a training issue? Maybe or maybe not. It depends on whether or not the owner wanted to take his dog patio dining. Notice that I said it was the owner's choice, not the dogs. In a better world, the dog would have a choice, too. Maybe that's why we love movies where dogs speak "human" and make choices. The next time you watch a movie that features dogs as main characters, make note of how often they are given cues versus how often they are free to make choices and then praised for making choices without human direction.

If the owner's goal is patio dining with his dog, then we start with training. But what if, after 6 months or so, the dog still can't behave while patio dining? Then, perhaps the dog is too overwhelmed by the stimuli, or perhaps the patio is too small for the dog to feel comfortable. Many patios are small. If the dog is in a corner, the tables are close together, or if there is a lot of foot traffic behind the dog, even the best-trained dog will feel uncomfortable.

The dog who is great at patio dining at one restaurant may struggle at a different one because the space is different. For larger dogs, this is a real concern. A 20- or 30-pound dog can learn to station under a chair. An 80-pound dog won't fit under a chair or table. They have no choice but to be in the walkway.

It's reasonable that Doggie Number 3, or any dog for that matter, simply doesn't enjoy patio dining (or any place we take them). Training is about skill acquisition. That's very different from temperament. Dogs can learn many skills. When and where the dog is comfortable performing those skills is different. Temperament, on the other hand, has more to do with the dog's preferences, tolerance levels, and resiliency. My dog can learn all the skills needed to hang out on a patio but not enjoy it. I could give her lots of high-value treats. She may enjoy the treats but not the dining experience. If I want to take her into a situation that she tolerates but doesn't necessarily enjoy, I need to be prepared to make sure I'm reinforcing her often with something she loves.

PLEASURE, TOLERANCE, AND DISLIKE . . . (NOT TODAY, MAYBE TOMORROW)

Have you ever just watched your dog when she's off-leash in a fenced area, like a yard or field? If your dog is given choices, what does she choose? Sniff the ground? Bring you a toy? Run the fence line? Bark? Lie in the grass and sunbathe? Dig? Run around you? Zoom around the yard? Go where you go? Does a perimeter check, then return to you or to a chosen observation spot? If you and your dog were hiking, what do you think your dog would do if given the choice between standing still and observing, trotting at her pace, or sniffing the ground or something else? That's difficult to predict, but through observation, we can gather clues and make some inferences. The answers to these questions depend on many different things, but the choices give us a clue. Discovering what her preferences are will help you understand her behavior.

If I'm going into the yard with my dog, she will run or trot outside, perform a general perimeter check (sniff the fence line, check out the chicken coop), stop to pee, sniff a bit more, check out what I'm doing, then find her spot (grass, deck, cot) and lie down. She usually stations herself within 10 feet of me.

If I'm eating, she'll come closer. If I have a cup of coffee, she stays in her spot. Ursa's preferred activity outside is observation. This is true when we go to new places, too. She's interested in discovering what's going on and keeping tabs on what I'm doing. Games we play generally involve us interacting with each other, like hide and seek or "follow me." If approached by strangers, her behavior is similar; check out the stranger, maybe engage, but maybe not, then station herself where she can observe. If she likes the person, then she can't seem to sniff them enough. It can be overwhelming for her new human friend! Based on her breed type, she's just about spot on for what I'd expect.

If approached by an unknown dog when she's on a leash, she will first observe. If the dog continues to come toward her, she will move away and sniff the ground. If the dog continues to move closer, her body will tense. If the dog gets 8–10 feet from us, Ursa will bark and try to move away. If she's in a fenced area, she'll keep a distance. Generally, Ursa needs to meet a dog several times before she decides if she'll engage with the dog. She has a few doggie friends, and that's all she needs.

Knowing what her preferences are helps me understand what kinds of activities she might prefer, what she might tolerate, and what she may not like. Activities that she would likely enjoy include lounging on the couch while I read, lounging in my office while I work, greeting people at the door and keeping an eye on them, hanging out in the yard observing her domain while I weed the garden, going for short car rides, doing parkour, and taking trips to the vet. That last one may surprise you. Ursa has never had a negative experience at the vet. Our vet has incredible patience with Ursa. Bonus: Ursa gets lots of her preferred kinds of attention there.

There are things that Ursa tolerates, like group training

classes. She'll perform (for the right paycheck), but group classes cannot accommodate her need to observe. Group classes require, for the most part, more doing and less watching. She'll tolerate it, but she doesn't enjoy it. Activities that are off the table for Ursa include going to community festivals, dog parks, and farmer's markets. Could I train her to go to some of those places? Possibly. Would she enjoy it? Probably not. Is it worth it for me to spend the necessary amount of time needed to teach her to go to many places? Not really. Her needs are met, and the size of her world is just right for her.

One of Ursa's doggie friends, Onyx, is up for any adventure. Patio dining? Yes. Hiking? Yep. New dogs? Sure. Cats? Check. Traveling? Let's go! But, sleeping in on the weekend, maybe spending the day lounging? She'll tolerate it and go along with it, but she'd rather be adventuring.

It may be difficult to determine what your dog enjoys versus what your dog tolerates. Is it the activity, or is it the reinforcer or motivator (being with you, playing with a toy, delicious treats)? Sometimes, it's hard to discern between the two. Knowing what your dog doesn't like and has difficulty tolerating is critical. This is where things can go very wrong for your dog.

Bo was a medium sized mixed breed who tolerated one or two kids who regularly played fetch with him. His enjoyment of playing fetch was more motivating than his desire to stay away from the kids. His family assumed that Bo liked kids. They had seen him play fetch many times with the neighbor kids. No one noticed that after a few repetitions of fetch, he stopped playing and went as far away from the kids as possible, maybe through the dog door and into the house. If anyone noticed that Bo went inside, it was assumed that he was tired.

During a family get-together, there were six kids at the house, more than the one or two kids he's used to. Bo had the freedom to be inside or outside. The belief was that the dog liked kids, so no one was monitoring the child-dog interaction. There was no discussion about how well the children understood how to interact with a dog safely.

Everything was fine for the first hour or so. Bo greeted the guests and played fetch a bit with the kids. Two of the children were chasing the dog. Everyone thought that was cute. They were playing so well. What a nice dog! Bo finally got away from the children and went inside the house. Everything was going so well! No one saw the child follow the dog into the house. No one saw the dog trying to get away from the child. No one saw the child cornering the dog or heard the dog growl. Everyone heard the child scream when the dog bit the child. I've heard similar scenarios from clients who contacted me after their dog bit a child. This is a tragic situation that can be avoided.

This dog tolerated children. That's very different from enjoying children. Being tolerant only gets you so far. At some point, it will be too much, and you will react. This is true for dogs, too. One of the challenges in this situation is that it's hard to wrap our heads around. We can't place fault on a single individual. It wasn't a single individual's fault; it was a combination of factors. It was the perfect storm, fueled by misunderstanding and assumption.

The next time you see your dog trainer, ask them how often they've seen family dogs who tolerated but didn't enjoy children, particularly children under 8 years old. I see it often. In general, once I point it out to the family, everyone makes adjustments. Most people, especially children, have no idea their dog doesn't like being hugged, patted on the head, or having a person come nose-to-nose with them. When children and dogs live together or spend time together, it's critical that children be taught how to be safe around dogs and that adults learn how to supervise child-dog interactions. If you have a dog and there are children in your life, I strongly encourage you to read Colleen Pelar's book *Living with Kids and Dogs Without Losing Your Mind.*

THE "SPOILED" DOG ... (MY DOG HAS EVERYTHING AND MORE)

I love buying things for my dogs. Does that mean my dogs are spoiled? No. It means I like buying things for my dogs. My dogs have nothing to do with my spending habits. It does mean that my dogs have a ridiculous number of toys, toy boxes, collars (a different one each month – don't judge me! I like a fashionable canine), a leash for every situation, enrichment/interactive toys, and dog beds. Part of my doggie spending is trying out new products to recommend to clients. But are my dogs spoiled? No. Neither dog asked for any of these things.

Being spoiled isn't just about stuff and fluff. It could include a dog who does as he pleases. Perhaps the dog sleeps in his guardian's bed or is allowed up on the furniture. I've even heard dogs being referred to as spoiled for being hand fed. Does this mean the dog thinks he's spoiled? Probably not.

People see the world through their perspective. That's valid. But we're trying to think about the world from our canine companion's perspective. Does a dog have a concept of being spoiled? I suspect dogs see things differently. I imagine that Ursa wants meaning and purpose in her life. What might that look like? She's part of the Guardian breed group defined in Kim Brophey's book *Meet Your Dog*. If she's living her best life, she'll engage in activities that include protective behavior, like barking, some degree of wariness (not fearfulness) of strangers, being gentle and compassionate with her social group (family, friends, household pets), independent, strong sense of appropriateness (i.e., bossy, can be the fun police), calm and relaxed most of the day until she's not, then she's large, loud, and in control.

When Ursa barks at something outside, and I let her, am I spoiling her, letting her get away with barking? No. When the kids were young and our Great Dane, Lucy, interrupted their boisterous play, should I have stopped her? No. She was maintaining calm and appropriate levels of arousing play (and it was darn funny). Does letting Ursa station herself on the couch so she has a better view out the window without first getting my permission mean letting her get away with whatever she wants? No. She's doing her doggie things. Sometimes, she barks, and I look outside, see absolutely nothing, and wonder, "Why does my dog do that?" Often the answer is that I just don't know.

We're taught culturally that giving in to a dog and letting them do what they want is spoiling them. The spoiled dog may just be a dog doing doggie things without unnecessary interruptions by the humans in her life.

What does living in a multi-species home look like? How can we meet each species' innate needs and find joy together? We can get curious. We can wonder, "Why does my dog do that?" and then think about it from their perspective. We can adjust our expectations, assuming that our dogs will act like dogs. Finding joy together may include implementing management strategies for safety, especially when children and dogs are involved. It also means learning to be comfortable with not knowing. Why does my dog bark at night when I don't see anything? It doesn't matter. Your dog knows something is amiss. You may never know why, but you can accept that it's part of her expression of normal dogginess.

9
A PLACE TO CALL HOME...
(HOME IS WHERE OUR HEART IS

P roviding housing may sound obvious, but humor me, and let's take a closer look. When you bring a dog into your life, you'll be sharing your home with a different species. Dogs, like people, are social. Too often, the conflict between human standards and normal dog behavior results in the dog being isolated. Some dogs are limited to living outside, spending little time with others of their own species, or interacting with their human family. They may have a doghouse, food, and water, but their well-being is poor. Imagine being both captive and isolated. Who wants a life like that? Dogs may be isolated to the basement, crate, kennel, or garage for many hours at a time. All the toys and chews in the world cannot replace social interaction. While their housing needs may be met technically, they are not living a quality life.

Living peacefully in a multi-species home takes some planning. A couple of years ago, we had the floors in our house redone. I spent hours learning about different types of floors, comparing flooring, and finally selecting something that a) I found aesthetically pleasing and b) would hold up to the wear and tear of giant dogs. The day finally arrived when the floors were finished. I was thrilled – they looked great. Then I promptly covered much of the flooring with runners and area rugs. If you studied the placement of the rugs in my home, you'd be able to identify a walking path, a trail of non-slip surfaces. The rugs are for the dogs, not me. Slippery flooring is not ideal for many dogs, especially dogs who have mobility problems, like my senior dog. On cleaning day, the rugs go into the washer, while my older guy generally stays upstairs, where the rooms are carpeted, and I enjoy the floors the way I'd envisioned them. Once the rugs are clean, they go back on the floor, and my senior boy comes back downstairs. The rugs are a small accommodation for his benefit.

Most homes have furniture for humans. Who has access to the furniture can be a source of tension in multi-species families. Some humans may not want the dog on the furniture, while others in the house may think it's fine. Some people have been told (erroneously) that dogs should never be allowed on furniture. That's a myth I'd really like to see vanish! In my home, the furniture is used by humans and dogs. The dogs also have access to furniture that the humans typically don't use, like dog beds and cots. Whether your dog is allowed on human furniture is a personal preference. It's not a right or wrong issue. If you don't want your dog to share human furniture, you need to provide an alternative, preferably near the areas where people spend most of their time. That may mean having several dog beds or cots in the house. But dogs are dogs; isn't lying on the floor good enough? Yes, however, if you don't want your dog on the furniture, a bed may decrease the struggle of keeping the dog off the furniture. Dogs, like people, may find a soft place to land more comfortable than the floor for napping.

Thinking about some of the reasons people don't allow

dogs on furniture brings up this point: dogs are dogs. They track dirt in the house. So do people. They shed. So do people (hair, skin – yep, we shed, too). As a mom of five children, I'm confident that I've spent more time cleaning up after human family members than the dogs. Spilled drinks, food on the floor, broken glasses, dirty laundry – cleaning up after people is much more work than wiping muddy paw prints or drool around the water bowl. When you add a dog to the mix of people in the house, it will get messier. There will be more mud, fur, and drool. I've met people who spent a lot of effort wiping paws at the door, each struggling with their dog because the dog doesn't like having paws cleaned. I've had clients whose dogs growled at them when getting their paws wiped. From your dog's perspective, muddy paws are normal, so why the fuss? Our canine companions simply do not understand the human desire for clean floors and fur-free furniture. This disconnect can cause tension between person and pet.

I'll admit – I'm a bit of a neat freak. I like order in my home. I dislike messiness. But I also enjoy living with other people and dogs. I've learned to adapt to some degree, and I've made adjustments in my environment to minimize muddy paws. At the front and back doors of our home, I have 5-foot-long rugs. Dogs (and people) coming into the house have to walk on the rug, which picks up a lot of dirt. It doesn't get all the dirt but gets most of it. We chose hard floors rather than wall-to-wall carpeting in the main living areas. Running the Bissell vacuum/mop combo weekly (or every other day during mud season) keeps things reasonably clean. I've put blankets where the dogs like to lie to protect the furniture. There is carpeting upstairs in the bedrooms and my office, so we invested in a carpet cleaner for the home. Cleaning supplies include enzyme cleaner, poop bags, and extra towels. The expectation is that things happen – diarrhea, vomit, pee – so be prepared.

However, the unexpected can slip up on you. I once had a foster dog who had severe nosebleeds. He was an older gentleman with serious health problems. Cleaning up after nosebleeds daily was exhausting, but I now have new tools in my cleaning kit. If I wanted to live in a home that was clean and organized to my liking, I would live alone – no people, no pets. But I do want people and pets in my life, so I've learned to make accommodations. It's not easy, but the benefits of those wonderful relationships are worth a little mud on the floor.

An update to the old saying, "Home is where the heart is," is needed. "Home is where our hearts are" – the humans and the dogs. It's more than sharing a space. It's the shared experience of the residents. It's what you make it. You decide if the dogs can lounge on the couch. It's not a moral decision. It's a "what's right for our home" decision. Resist other people's list of dos and don'ts. Discover what works for your home. Sure, there are accommodations we make to meet the needs of others, like adding non-slip rugs to help our senior dogs move around better. And, yes, the house will be messier. Make a plan and have cleaning supplies at hand. Expect the mess. Home is where we share life and make memories with the others in our dwelling, both human and canine.

10

LISTENING WITH UNDERSTANDING…(YOUR DOG ISN'T LISTENING TO YOU AND YOU MAY NOT BE LISTENING TO YOUR DOG)

Communication between two people is complex. Cross-species communication is even more challenging. We may understand what we mean, but do other people? Do our dogs? Maybe not. Words are human inventions to facilitate better communication. Humans are not born knowing words. Humans learn the meanings of words over time. We then spend years in school learning grammar rules so our use of words can be understood by other humans. The point is that it's unrealistic to expect your dog, who has not had the benefit of 12 or more years of learning words and language rules, to understand human language.

Many words we use daily can only be understood by knowing the context. Words can have multiple meanings based on the context the word is used. No is a good example. What does "no" mean? What do I mean if I walk into the kitchen and say, "No"? How would you discover the answer? Context is key.

. . .

From the *Oxford Languages Online,* "no" is defined as 1) not any (determiner); 2) used to give a negative response (exclamation); 3) not at all (adverb). Based on these definitions, the word "no" is not a behavior. Performing "no" makes no sense. When the dog is told, "No," what behavior should she perform? Cues given imply an action is expected. When we say, "Sit" to our dog, it's easy to see if the dog performed correctly. When we tell the dog, "No," how do we know if the dog performed "no" correctly? If "no" cannot be performed, what should a dog do when told, "No"? From the dog's perspective, "no" is just another of the thousands of noises a human makes throughout the day. "No" may be associated with an angry, potentially aggressive human. The dog may actually associate the sound "no" with fear in general, or worse, fear of you.

Do I say, "No" to my dogs? Occasionally. What do I mean when I say, "No"? Usually, when I say, "No" to my dogs, I'm being reactive. You could say that I'm barking at the dog! Even as the word rolls off my tongue, I follow it with what I want them to do. I don't expect them to respond to the word no, but if I'm lucky, it may interrupt them while I'm fumbling around trying to decide what I want them to do. For example, maybe I left my hard-boiled egg on the table while I went upstairs to find my ringing phone. I answer the phone, talk for a few minutes, hang up, and remember my egg. I go downstairs just in time to see Ursa lick the egg. Gross! I have an instant reaction – "NO!" She looks at me, but not because she feels guilty for doing something wrong. She looks at me because I startled her. She's likely to go right back to the egg if I don't ask her to do something else. At that moment, I have several options. I can ask her to lie down, back up, come to me, go to her bed. Those are useful instructions because she knows what those cues mean, and I can immediately see whether she performed the task correctly. "No" is not something I can teach because it's not an action she can take.

The best that can be said for "no" is that it interrupts the undesirable behavior. Interrupting the undesirable behavior is fine. There are many ways to interrupt, like a quick clap of your hands, or whistling. When you need to interrupt a behavior, avoid scaring your dog. Creating fear can decrease the quality of life, increase stress, and damage trust. Using fear to manage undesirable behavior communicates one thing: people are unpredictable and potentially dangerous. Often, when we're presented with a situation that needs interrupting, we forget a very powerful option: a cued behavior. It takes practice. First, you need to practice some simple tasks that become so ingrained that your dog responds without pausing to think about it. Hand target (dog touches person's hand with her snout) is one of my favorites. Ursa hand targets with enthusiasm. Another of my top picks is *back up*. Second, you need to remember to ask your dog to do something else. In the moment of panic, when your first response is "no," take a moment and instead try asking your dog to do something, anything, else.

GRAMMAR ISN'T PART OF THE PUPPY CLASS CURRICULUM . . . (MAYBE IT SHOULD BE)

Adjectives help create vivid mental images. People use them to amplify meaning. Adjectives create word pictures.

- I went for a walk.
- I walked for an hour.
- I took an hour-long walk in the park.

- One cool fall morning, I meandered through the
  woods for an hour, exhilarated by the crisp air,
  dazzled by the rich colors of the fall leaves

Adjectives are helpful because we've assigned meaning and
value to them. I can create tranquility or horror with words.
But that only works if I use the words appropriately and my
audience understands the words and their function. But does
my dog understand adjectives or any word modifiers?

Good is a common modifier people use when talking about
dogs. "He's a good dog." "I just want my dog to be good." What
does good mean? When people use the word "good" when
talking about a dog, I interpret it as meaning the dog follows
the rules. The dog is compliant. The dog doesn't do doggie
things like jumping, barking, digging, or chewing. The dog
doesn't do much, just lies around and doesn't get into things.
The dog may also be fearful, anxious, shut down, or stressed
out. Does the dog feel like he's good or has a good quality of
life? What does good mean from the dog's perspective? If the
dog isn't good, does that make the dog bad?

People also use the word good when talking to their dogs.
"Good girl!" "Good sit." Does your dog understand good as a
modifier? What's the difference between *sit* and "good sit"? I
often wonder what goes through a dog's mind when she's told
sit followed by "good" followed by *sit*. Cue, followed by praise,
followed by the cue a second time. How confusing that must
be! Most trainers will tell people to say the cue one time, yet
the cue is repeated as part of praise. Good as a modifier may
not make any sense to your dog. If your dog is praised ("Good!"
or "Good girl!") after a correct performance, that may be easier
to understand than a cue followed by a modifier plus the cue.
Remember, puppy classes teach performance, not grammar.

CLEAR COMMUNICATION . . . (ACTIONS ARE LOUDER THAN WORDS)

Like most dog owners, I talk to my dogs. I deliver long-winded soliloquies often. My dogs seem to be able to tell whether I'm chattering away at no one in particular or talking to them. A clear indicator that I'm trying to engage is my tone of voice. My cheerful, chirpy voice invites adventure ("Wanna go for a walk?" . . . "Wanna jump over the log?" . . . "Wanna go for a car ride?" . . . "Wanna play?"). A big sigh, followed by a questioning tone, causes Ursa to watch me (sigh . . . "Really, did you have to do that?"). I don't know why. If I use my stern mom's voice, she'll freeze, make herself smaller, or go to another room. That's not the way to get her to come back to me! If I startle and make a noise (squeal, exclaim), she barks. Communication between a person and a pet happens all the time. No words are needed. Dogs are masters at reading our body language, predicting our actions, and understanding our emotional state without us ever uttering a word. That's part of what makes treating separation anxiety so difficult. We can't sneak out of the house. Our dogs know we're getting ready to leave the house well before we actually walk out the door. We can't fool our dogs.

Without a single word, we can send a dog into a panic. Communication is a two-way interaction. Putting a hand out to pet a dog's head can be interpreted as a threat and invoke a fear response (ducking or moving away). You may think you're being friendly, but the dog may think differently. Dogs and people use space to communicate. If I step into my dog's space, she may step back, turn away, or lean into me for affection. My dog may come into my space seeking affection or trying to engage in play. I may respond by stepping back, telling her to back up, or giving her the affection or play she's seeking.

EFFECTIVE CROSS-SPECIES COMMUNICATION . . . (LET'S GET TO KNOW EACH OTHER)

Think about a time when you met someone who became a close friend, a roommate, or a partner. How much time did you spend getting to know them? Was your first concern getting them to comply with your requests, or was it learning to understand and communicate with them? When you brought your canine companion home, what was your first goal, compliance or getting to know her?

It's time for a trainer confession. My dogs generally don't sit to get their meals unless they choose to. *Sit* isn't important in my house. I'm less interested in training my puppy than I am in playing with her and discovering what she likes. We may play nosework games, play hide-and-seek, experiment with different toys (remember, I LOVE buying things for my dogs), and spend time just being together. Yes, I want her to pee outside rather than inside. Yes, I want her to resist the temptation to counter-surf. Yes, I want her to stay in the yard, come when called, and walk politely on a leash. But those skills can be taught anytime. When I bring a new dog home, I want to get to know her. I want to help her adjust to our home and our schedule. Really, I just want to sit and watch her. Plenty of time to learn rules as we go.

When I bring a new puppy home, I don't presume to know anything about her. By now, you know I'm partial to Great Danes. I will still need to get to know the next Great Dane puppy I bring home. Yes, I know the breed's general characteristics and developmental phases, but that doesn't mean I know the puppy sitting in front of me. Every pup is an individual. The time I invest in getting to know my dog – how she interacts with new things, her preferences, her tolerance to change, and how resilient she is – helps me understand her. It helps me know how to meet her specific needs. I can identify areas where she needs a little more help. Letting her make choices can help me identify potential reinforcers, which will make training faster and more fun for her.

When we go to puppy class, the focus is generally teaching the puppy how to conform to our standards. A lot of time is spent teaching the dog to do what we tell her to do. But how much time is spent learning what the dog is saying, and what she's communicating? Dog owners need to spend as much, or possibly more, time learning to understand canine communication. Understanding your dog's natural language can prevent many problem behaviors. For example, you're out walking your puppy. He suddenly stops and refuses to move forward. You coax. You try treats to lure him forward. You pull at the leash. Finally, in exasperation, you pick the puppy up and move along. You may think your puppy is stubborn. Or stupid. Your puppy really wishes you understood that he was saying he was scared. We may not be able to identify what caused the puppy to become frightened: a sound, an odor, a moving object, or a texture on the ground. But, at that moment, your puppy was communicating. Over time, the puppy may grow too big to pick up. That initial refusal to move forward may turn into lunging and barking while on a leash.

Let's try that a different way. You and your puppy are on a walk. You notice your puppy is lagging behind you. You wonder if he's tired already. Then he stops. He won't budge, not even for the chicken in your hand. You pause – is it safe to stop, or do we really need to move? You look around. You can't identify anything out of the ordinary. Maybe, you think, we should turn around and go back. Great idea! When you approach your puppy, you calmly say, "Let's go this way," while turning around. At first, your puppy doesn't move, so you pause for a moment. Then he gets up. You notice that his nose goes up a little – is he sniffing the air? He takes a step toward you. You offer a piece of chicken. Yes! He takes it. Now, the two of you are walking slowly, and then, as if by magic, he's back to his normal pace, and things seem to be fine. Interesting, you think. I wonder what happened?

The next day, you and your puppy head out for a walk. You take the same route you did the day before. The entire pattern repeats. This time, though, you are watching your puppy. You notice that he started slowing down two houses earlier on your path. You repeat the pattern from the day before and head back home.

On the third day, you and your puppy are on your walk just like you were the last two days. As you approach the spot where your puppy has been slowing down, then freezing, you notice your neighbor rolling out their trash can to the curb. Your puppy stops, lies down, and starts trembling when he hears the trash can being wheeled out. Then you remember that last week on trash day, your puppy was startled when passing this house. Your puppy started anticipating the scary thing – the trash can – two houses earlier. Usually, your puppy is inside when you take the trash out. He's never seen a rolling trash can. This is an opportunity to help the puppy learn that trash day is okay. You've identified something your puppy needs help with, and your puppy has learned to trust that you'll listen and protect him from danger. Cookies for everyone!

LET'S TALK . . . (TIME WELL SPENT)

When we bring a new dog home, too often, we're in a rush to do everything all at once. I'm giving you permission to slow down. Relax. Take a cue from your dog – time spent observing, sniffing, and exploring is good. Skills can be learned at any age.

But taking time to really understand what your dog enjoys and to see through your dog's eyes can't be rushed. If you asked me what's more important, playing with your dog in the backyard or going to a group class, I'd say, given the choice, play. Play is a great way to teach life skills like *wait, recall,* and *drop it.* Your dog is learning even if you don't incorporate cues into play sessions.

Even if you've had dogs for years, you and your new companion will benefit from learning together. You've never had the dog sitting in front of you. Sometimes, we need to make choices with our time and money. There are many ways to provide training. Going to three or four group classes may not be realistic for your home situation. You many only need help with one or two things. In that case, hiring a private trainer is more efficient than going to a group class that may not address your specific need. Although more costly upfront, private training is the most effective for teaching you and your dog how to live together successfully.

My dog doesn't listen to me. Your dog thinks you don't listen to her. Tensions rise, and conflict between human and canine happens. And everyone is unhappy. Listening and understanding are skills that both human and canine develop over time as they get to know each other, spend time together, and learn to trust each other. Dogs aren't born knowing human language, and people aren't born understanding canine language. So, slow down. Take time to learn about each other. Play together. Develop that relationship. The stronger the relationship, the clearer the communication. I believe that. The relationship is the foundation for clear, consistent communication and, its corollary, trust. Do those first; we can teach skills along the way.

11

PLAY WITH YOUR DOG...
(PEOPLE NEED TO PLAY, TOO)

P lay keeps us young mentally and physically. The same is true for our dogs. People often remark that their older dog started playing more when they added a puppy to the family. I've seen this in my own home.

It seems natural to play with our puppies. Playing with a puppy is fun until those shark teeth miss the toy and clamp onto your hand. Ouch, that hurts! When your bitey puppy clamps down on your fingers, and it will happen, that in no way means your puppy is aggressive. Why don't I think that bitey puppies are aggressive? When my children were infants and bit me with those sharp baby teeth, I never thought the baby was aggressive, even though it hurt. Puppies, like human babies and toddlers, explore the world with their mouths. Anything that is flapping about (pant legs, hands, curtains) looks like a toy. Walking through the house in your most comfortable pair of sweatpants doesn't seem that interesting to you. But your puppy sees a potential toy. So, he clamps on. Then, oh, what fun, instant game of tug happens, so your puppy thinks. You're just trying to get your pant leg out of puppy's mouth.

I've experienced, and many of my clients have, too, walking through the house and being grabbed by a bitey puppy. Guess what? It got my attention! Sometimes, that bitey behavior is reinforced accidentally. Here's the sequence of events: puppy needs our attention, but we're unaware of the need. Puppy grabs a pant leg, shoe, or hand with their shark-like teeth (remember, they don't have hands). We stop – Ouch! And give our puppy attention. Puppy thinks, "Wow! Grabbing my human with my mouth works!" And there we have it – the classic "bitey puppy gets our attention" behavior sequence. My ego will not permit me to admit just how many times I've found myself undoing that particular behavior sequence. Just because I'm a professional trainer does not negate the fact that I'm still a human navigating life in a multi-species home and wondering, "Why did I do that?" after asking myself, "Why did my puppy do that?"

Tired puppies also tend to be grabby-bitey. Your sweet puppy who went to the vet and the pet store may be more grabby-bitey later in the day. Overstimulated and short on rest, your pup has less impulse control. Chewing or bitey behavior may be one way for her to soothe herself. For tired pups, time spent in a pen or crate with a chew toy is a good solution.

Bitey behavior tends to creep into playtime. Those shark-like puppy teeth clamping onto a hand decrease our desire to play with our puppies. When we are less likely to play, our puppies may become more insistent, more demanding, and more bitey. If we're not having fun playing with our puppy, then we stop playing. So, the puppy tries harder to engage with us. And we become more frustrated. No one wins.

Puppies learn about their world and develop physically through play. It's a critical need for development. Appropriate play can prevent undesirable behavior, like furniture chewing, shoe stealing, and mouthiness.

When playing with our dogs, we must remember that our dog is a dog. We're having an inter-species moment. Human play and dog play are different. Our goal is to adjust play to meet the needs for fun and safety for both human and canine.

DOG VS. HUMAN . . . (HOW DO WE PLAY?)

When was the last time you caught a disc (i.e., Frisbee) with your mouth? Or grabbed a ball in your mouth and ran? How about snagging a tug toy in your mouth and shaking it at your dog? Never? Does your dog think it odd that you don't play tug with your mouth? When my dog uses her paws when we're playing tug, is she mimicking how I use my arms?

Play between the species is different primarily because our bodies are physiologically different. I've been nipped during tug sessions, usually by young, bitey puppies still learning to keep their teeth off my flesh. Is the pup trying to cause pain? No. Is the puppy bad? No. An accidental nip can leave a mark or puncture on me that wouldn't leave a mark on another dog because the dog has fur protecting his skin. I can solve this problem by wearing a long-sleeved sweatshirt. Or by taking a play break before puppy gets too wound up.

How often and what kind of play you engage in depends on you and your dog. As dogs get older, the intensity of play changes, but preferences remain the same. The intensity and duration of a game of tug with a 12-week-old puppy is much lower than a game of tug with an 18-month-old adolescent. That same dog will still enjoy tug when they are 10 years old, but the intensity and duration of the game will be lower than at any previous time in life.

SETTING UP FOR SUCCESS . . . (KEEPING IT FUN FOR EVERYONE)

Safety first, in play and life, is a great way to prevent problems, especially during inter-species play. One of the simplest ways to keep things safe is moderating excitement. When dogs or people get too amped up, things can get out of control quickly.

PRINCIPLE #1: PLAY IN BURSTS

When playing tug, I'm particularly aware of my dog's teeth. Those pearly whites are made for ripping and shredding tough things like animal hides and crunching bones. I really don't want them connecting with my sensitive human skin! We tug in short bursts, generally 3–5 seconds at a time. One of us will offer the tug toy, the other will grab it, and we tug. At the end of the 3–5 seconds, I drop the toy, say, *all done* and pause for 2–3 seconds. If we both want to continue playing, then I offer the toy again, usually saying something like, "Wanna tug?" Then, we repeat the play cycle. Playing in short bursts helps me gauge my dog's level of excitement. We're having fun, but no one is out of control.

PRINCIPLE #2: ASK PERMISSION

There are times when I want to play with my dog. I may look at my calendar and think, "I've got 10 minutes before I need to leave. I'll play with Ursa before I go." If I grab her favorite toy and offer it to her, she has the option to decline. If she declines, then I go do something else.

At times, when my dog asks me to play, I also have the option to decline. When I'm not willing to play, I communicate that to her. That prevents undesirable attention seeking. If playing with me isn't an option, I may tell her to get her bone. When she was a puppy, I would give her something to do, like a treat ball, busy box, or long-lasting chew. That gave her something to do that didn't require interaction with me.

PRINCIPLE #3: CHOOSE THE RIGHT TOY

Pet stores offer an overwhelming number of toys for dogs. Most are pleasing to the human eye (great marketing!). But how many toys are really good for humans and dogs to use when playing together? That question narrows it down quite a bit.

If I want to play tug with my dog, I want a lot of distance between my hand and my dog's mouth. Why? I don't want her heavy-duty canine chompers anywhere near my frail human hand! My preferred tug toy is 3 feet long. That keeps my hand safe while we have a great game of tug.

Catching a disc is another game many dogs love. I'm thrilled to see a variety of safe, non-splintering discs on the market. When choosing a disc, I like to find something that contrasts with the environment to make it easier to see, like bright yellow or orange. Some discs are designed for dogs to easily pick them up off the ground without pawing at them.

PRINCIPLE #4: ENCOURAGE INDEPENDENT PLAY

If I give my dog a tug toy, she needs me to play with her. A tug toy without a friend to tug with is no fun. What about toys that don't require human interaction? Jolly Balls are a top favorite for my dogs. They can whip the ball around by the rope, tossing it in the air, then chase and grab it. Tether tug toys are another option. A flexible pole stuck in the ground with a tug attached is fun for dogs who really enjoy tug. Hide-

A-Squirrel is an all-time favorite for all my dogs! I stuff the squeaky squirrels inside the plush log and put it in the toy box. When Ursa wants to play and I can't, I'll tell her to go find her squirrel. She spends 10 minutes or more playing with her Hide-A-Squirrel. She loves it so much that when I saw a Hide-A-Dinosaur (small dinosaur squeaky toy inside a big plush egg), I bought it. Hands down, that's her favorite toy of all time. Like the Jolly Ball, the Hide-A-Dinosaur promotes independent play.

Quiet play is important, too. When Ursa digs through one of the toy boxes and chooses a hard toy (bull horn, bone, antler), I know exactly what will happen next. She'll find a comfy spot, usually a dog bed, and she'll settle down and chew for a while. Then she'll take a long nap. Her toy boxes are filled with options that let her choose the level of activity that meets her current needs. In short, your dog's toy box needs a variety of toys, including interactive toys to encourage play with you, toys they can play with on their own, and toys they can relax with, like hard chews.

KIDS AND DOGS . . . (SAFETY FIRST AND ALWAYS)

The trainer part of me says all child-dog interactions should be supervised. There are good reasons for this perspective. First, children are unable to recognize when a dog is getting too excited. That's actually true for many adults, too. Second, when play gets too exciting, and the dog starts jumping, leaping, or getting mouthy, children do exactly the wrong thing to try to calm things down. Yelling, squealing, screaming, flailing arms in the air, and running are natural responses kids have when they play with dogs. Those are exactly the behaviors that will increase arousal and intensify a dog's behavior. So, the adult in the house hears the child screaming, has no idea what's actually going on, sees the dog running amok, and scolds the dog. The version I usually hear usually includes phrases like "The dog is too aggressive when playing with the kids." No, the dog is not being aggressive. The dog is excited and doing what dogs do: running, leaping, and chasing. The child is excited and doing what kids do: running, squealing, and flailing their arms. The real issue here is that the interaction was too much for either child or dog to handle on their own.

Okay, the mom part of me says it's good for the kids and dog to play. They can burn off energy with each other while I'm working on one of the hundred things on my to-do list. I can't keep my eyes on everyone all the time. It'll be fine if the kids aren't being mean to the dog. Yes, that exact thought went through my head dozens of times when my children were young. If memory serves, four of the five kids got nipped at some point by a dog or a cat in our house. Everyone got scratched by a dog or a cat. Being nipped is different than being bitten. Getting nipped during play is not the same issue as being nipped when the dog is scared and growling. A herding-type dog that is nipping the heels of the running children is probably not being aggressive, and they are performing species-specific behavior: herding the chaotic beings and trying to get everyone to calm down. Unfortunately, most people, particularly children, don't understand the nuances of dog communication. How do we keep everyone safe while fostering these important inter-species relationships and experiences? The trainer in me got together with the mom in me over a hot cup of coffee and developed some practical safety tips for you.

SETTING UP SAFE CHILD-DOG PLAY

Dogs and children share some common play games, like chasing games. Young children especially seem to love chasing and being chased. Dogs do, too. This normal, fun-filled game burns energy, sending kids into fits of giggles, and invigorating the family dog. It's quite entertaining. Until the puppy accidentally knocks over the child. It can be scary when a 30-, 40-, 50-, or 100-pound puppy knocks over a 4- or 5-year-old child. These things happen even when play is supervised. It's no one's fault. Getting angry that the puppy was playing with the child isn't logical.

What often does happen is the dog is expected to "know better," as if dogs are born understanding the complexities of human behavior and the fragility of children. Expecting the non-human species (aka your dog) to understand how to play gently with a toddler or child is unrealistic. If the child is too young to recognize that the dog is getting too excited, then the general rule of thumb is that the child is too young to interact with the dog without active supervision. That means the adult in the home needs to be actively involved in the interaction. Here's an example. When my grandson, Rodger, was about 2 years old, my Great Dane puppy was about 8 months old. Ursa weighed just over 100 pounds. Rodger weighed about 28 pounds. Rodger was afraid of Ursa when she was zooming in the house or when she would try to get him to play with her. That was completely understandable. Teaching Ursa and Rodger how to interact required the three of us play together.

One of the games we played was toss the toy. Rodger and I would gather all of Ursa's toys onto the couch while Ursa was outside. Once Rodger was safely on the couch, surrounded by toys, I let Ursa inside and walked her to the living room. I sat next to Rodger and told him to throw a toy away from Ursa as far as he could. I didn't want Ursa to think that Rodger was throwing the toy at her. The goal of the game was to toss a toy behind or to the side of Ursa when she was trotting or running toward Rodger and me while we sat on the couch. Once Ursa caught on – when she approached the couch, a toy would fly through the air, and she could chase and grab it – she started pausing before she got to the couch to see which way the toy would go. Once Rodger realized that Ursa wasn't going to pounce on him to get the toy, he started laughing out loud when Ursa got the toy. Five minutes of the toy toss was enough activity for Ursa, so she'd go take a nap. Sometimes, she curled up on the couch near Rodger to nap while he watched TV.

In the kitchen, I'd put Rodger on the kitchen counter or at the table with a jar of treats. We'd play the same kind of game: Rodger tossed a treat away from Ursa. She learned that keeping her distance earned a treat. Rodger learned how to keep Ursa from getting too close. The dog and child were learning to share space safely.

Helping children and dogs play safely does take planning and training. Children seem to enjoy playing soccer-type games with their dogs. First, teach your dog to nose or paw at a soccer ball to get it to move. Once the dog is moving the ball consistently, introduce moving the ball for some distance, say 6 to 10 feet. Next, add moving the ball to a target or goal. The goalie (your child) can then toss the ball out of the goal to repeat the game.

Sometimes, it's necessary to implement a management plan when the kids want to actually play soccer. A sudden change of rules –playing keep-away from the dog – could create problems. If the kids are using their feet to kick the ball away from the dog, the dog could accidentally get kicked. That could cause the dog to defend herself from the kick or teach the dog to be afraid of the kids. Better to keep your dog inside with a nice chew toy or enrichment activity during backyard soccer matches.

While we don't want children to be injured by or afraid of the dog when playing, we also want to prevent the dog from being injured by or afraid of the children during play. Most people don't want their dog to chase children but don't give it much thought if the kids are chasing the dog. In some situations, chase games can be safe for kids and dogs, but that's not universally true. Letting a child chase a dog while the child is riding a bike, a scooter, or a battery-operated car is never acceptable. It's very difficult to identify at what point the chase shifts from fun for the dog to the dog feeling like he's in danger. The potential for accidentally running into the dog while on a bike or scooter is real. If a child hit a dog with a bike and the dog then bit the child, who would be at fault? Who would be punished? In my experience, the dog is almost always punished for biting, even though, from the dog's perspective, he was the one who was in danger and was defending himself. In the midst of the high emotions surrounding a child who was bitten by a dog, we don't often have the emotional capacity to stop and think about what might have happened. We're too busy reacting. Why take the risk?

Children running around and yelling is normal play behavior for kids. Some dogs try to join in the fun, sometimes knocking children over. Other dogs try to bring order to the chaos by herding, sometimes nipping at the children to get them to move to one spot and calm down. Several years ago, one of my Great Danes would interrupt the children by getting between them and barking at them until they calmed down if she felt the play was getting too rambunctious. Not bad behavior, but it might be undesirable. Although to be honest, I appreciated my Great Dane for keeping the over-the-top play in check. What would you like for the dog to do while the children play loudly? If your choice is anything other than species-typical behavior, you need to teach your dog what to do as well as have a management plan in place.

Play with your dog. Every. Single. Day. Learn how to play with your dog. Use play to get to know each other. Dogs help us be more playful. I'm sure I look ridiculous doing my mock playbow to Ursa, but when I do, her eyes light up, her body gets wiggly, and she playbows back. Except when she doesn't. Then we don't play. But when she does, it is magical to me. I mean that sincerely – it's magical. It is a shared experience that I can't quite describe. Does that mean play is a free-for-all? No. We have established play rules to keep everyone safe. I'm always aware of Ursa's level of excitement. Too much excitement might lead to me getting hurt, and I don't want that. Then we couldn't play while I recovered. Safe play is particularly important when kids and dogs play. Teaching children how to play and then actively supervising child-dog play sessions keeps everyone safe, happy, and eager to play together.

12

LIVING YOUR BEST LIFE... TOGETHER

Here we are, at the end of the book, but maybe at the beginning of your life together – human and canine. Regardless of what kind of dog you share life with, she is a dog first and always. Like the humans you share life with, your dog is unique, with thoughts, feelings, goals, and needs. She's quirky in her own lovable way. In spite of her "dogginess," you love her, and I hope you see her more clearly.

Our dogs are dogs. They annoy and delight us. They share our burdens. They light up the darkest of our days. We annoy and delight them. We are their source, the ones tasked with meeting their doggie needs. This is the interspecies relationship we label dog ownership. Is it really ownership? Not really. It's living life together, dog and human, experiencing things together from unique perspectives.

You are the gateway to the world for your canine companion. It's a heavy, sometimes burdensome, responsibility. At the end of a long day, when you get home (or walk out of your home office), there he is, waiting for you, needing to spend time with you, completely dependent on you to meet his needs. Are you up for the task? Most days, the answer is a resounding "Yes!" Some days, it's a struggle, but you manage. On rare days, you have nothing left to give, but somehow, looking into those adoring eyes, you find a little bit left to give after all. Our dogs inspire us to be the best human we can be.

Here's to you and your canine companion. Grab a special "I love you" cookie and give it to your dog. Have a great tug session. Go on a "sn-outing," and let your dog's nose guide your time outside. See the world through your dog's eyes. And, finally, here's your pass: perfection isn't necessary for a life well lived. Enjoy your dog for the amazing being she is – muddy paws, drool, and all.

RESOURCES

Brophey, Kim. *Meet Your Dog: The Game-Changing Guide to Understanding Your Dog's Behavior.* Chronicle Books, 2018.

Cook, A. *Play Way Dogs.* Accessed November 3, 2023. http://playwaydogs.com.

Gibeault, S. Dogs "Don't Have a Sixth Sense, They Just Have Incredible Hearing," American Kennel Club, July 13, 2018. https://www.akc.org/expert-advice/lifestyle/sounds-only-dogs-can-hear/

McConnell, Patricia. *The Education of Will: Healing a Dog, Facing My Fears, Reclaiming My Life.* Atria, 2018.

McConnell, Patricia. *The Other End of the Leash: Why We Do What We Do Around Dogs.* Ballantine Books, 2003.

Mellor, David J. "Updating animal welfare thinking: Moving beyond the "Five Freedoms" towards "a Life Worth Living"." *Animals* 6, no. 3 (2016): 21.

Mills, Daniel S., Isabelle Demontigny-Bédard, Margaret Gruen, Mary P. Klinck, Kevin J. McPeake, Ana Maria Barcelos, Lynn Hewison, et al. "Pain and problem behavior in cats and dogs." *Animals* 10, no. 2 (2020): 318.

Pelar, Colleen. *Living with Kids and Dogs... Without Losing Your Mind: A Parent's Guide to Controlling the Chaos.* Dream Dog Productions, 2012

Raffan, Eleanor, Rowena J. Dennis, Conor J. O'Donovan, Julia M. Becker, Robert A. Scott, Stephen P. Smith, David J. Withers et al. "A deletion in the canine POMC gene is associated with weight and appetite in obesity-prone Labrador retriever dogs." *Cell metabolism* 23, no. 5 (2016): 893-900.

www.ingramcontent.com/pod-product-compliance
Lightning Source LLC
Chambersburg PA
CBHW060524130626
46553CB00002B/634

* 9 7 9 8 9 8 9 6 8 4 6 0 1 *